Copyright © 2025 by Mike Kunert

All rights reserved.

No portion of this book may be reproduced in any form without written permission from the publisher or author, except as permitted by U.S. copyright law.

About This Book

I spent the first decade of my life growing up in Loma Linda. Like everything else you look back on as the years go by, I wish I had realized then what a good time I was having and found ways to soak up even more of it. To me, the 1950s were the best time to be a kid.

America was hands down the best country in the world. California was the best state in that country. And if you narrowed it down even further, the Inland Empire was the best part of California. Where else could you be only about an hour from the desert, the mountains, the ocean, Disneyland—and, if you felt like it, even the big city?

Back then, the Inland Empire was carpeted with orange groves, stretching almost as far as you could see. They're gone now, but in those days, we were living in what I can only call halcyon days. The whole Inland Empire was a wonderful place to live, but I happened to be centered in Loma Linda, and that shaped everything for me.

Even after I moved to Mentone in the 1960s, the center of my world always came back to Loma Linda. That stayed true until I finally left California in the mid-1990s.

This book is my way of remembering the people, places, and things that made those years special. Most of the chapters are written in my own voice, from my own memories. About a quarter of them were contributed by guest authors, also in the first person, which makes the stories feel all the more real.

Some of the chapters go back to events that happened before my time, and for those I had to lean on research. I've done my best to be as accurate as possible, though anyone working with seventy-year-old memories knows they're not always as sharp as they once were. Wherever I could, I checked and double-checked the facts to be sure the story was told right.

Through it all, one thing never changed—I've always been grateful that I grew up in Loma Linda, and for the friends and neighbors who shared that time with me. That gratitude is what this book is really about.

Special Thanks & Acknowledgments

A book like this doesn't come together on its own. It takes the help of friends, neighbors, and people who care about keeping memories alive. I owe a special debt of gratitude to all those who stepped in to share their stories, their pictures, and their encouragement along the way.

First, to the **guest authors**. Each of you gave not only your time but also your memories, and in some cases your family photographs. You made this book a richer, more personal collection than I could have ever created by myself. To be fair, I've listed you here in alphabetical order by last name, so no one thinks I'm putting one person ahead of another:

- Vicki and Kandy Bartlett
- Patti and Jenny Cotton
- Dawn Graves
- Nancy Magi
- Robert Peterson
- Margi Dalgleish Roth
- Emery Rockwell

- Genie Nelson Sample
- Scott Smith
- Betty Wieland

Thank you for letting your voices join mine in remembering Loma Linda.

I also want to acknowledge the organizations and individuals who allowed me to use photographs from their collections. Pictures bring history to life in a way that words alone can't, and I'm grateful for the doors that were opened to me:

- **Loma Linda University Department of Archives and Special Collections (Including cover credit)**
- **Loma Linda Parks and Historical Society**
- **Dixie Wheeler Plata of Wheeler's Photography**
- **California Department of Transportation**

And to the guest authors who furnished their own photographs, thank you as well. Your images added a personal touch that connected your memories directly to the reader.

To all of you—thank you for helping me tell this story. The memories of Loma Linda are brighter because you chose to share them.

Contents

1. LLU Helicopter Flight Nurse — 1
2. First National Bank of Loma Linda. — 11
3. Dr. Leonard Bailey — 14
4. Elder Wayne White — 22
5. Ritchie Mansion — 25
6. Loma Linda Chocolate Prune Cake-Recipe and Stories — 30
7. Phil the Plumber — 36
8. The Granary — 42
9. Milton Corwin — 45
10. Hazels Beauty Bar — 50
11. The Hippy Mailman of Loma Linda — 55
12. Peterson Tract — 64
13. Dick Schaefer — 71
14. Nelson Plumbing — 79

15.	The Emmersons and the Bartletts	85
16.	Smitty the Barber	92
17.	The Story of Pigeon Pass Road	100
18.	Ben Ruckle	111
19.	KDUO	114
20.	The School of Tropical and Preventive Medicine	116
21.	Roy Jutzy	125
22.	Backstory of Loma Linda Community Hospital	131
23.	Wall of Water	137
24.	The Slater Family	141
25.	Van Unger	149
26.	Dr. Ellsworth Wareham and the Heart Team	156
27.	The Vegetable Truck and Other Forgotten Luxuries	162
28.	Dr. George	169
29.	Emenel	175
30.	The LLU UFO	183
31.	The Pool (aka The Plunge)	187

32.	Gene White	193
33.	Lupe's Azteca Inn	199
34.	Wallace Koehl	204
35.	Clarence Harlow	208
36.	Here Is the Church, Here Is the Steeple...	213
37.	Campus Snack Shop	220
38.	How La Sierra College almost ended up in Yucaipa	223
39.	The Great Loma Linda Academy Fire of 1947	226
40.	Moving Day	230
41.	Hulda	240
42.	Herluf Jensen	248
43.	LLU Trust Dept.	253
44.	John Burden and $38,900	259
45.	The Great Flood of 1969	263
46.	I (also) Remember Loma Linda	274
Index		283

Chapter 1
LLU Helicopter Flight Nurse

By Dawn Graves

Photo Credit: Dawn Graves

When I reflect on my time as one of the first flight nurses for Loma Linda Medical Center's pioneering helicopter program, I'm struck by the profound mixture of excitement, challenge, and camaraderie that defined those early days. It all started in May 1972, when Loma Linda launched the first hospital-based helicopter program in the United States. I graduated from nursing school at Loma Linda that same month and had no inkling that my career trajectory was about to take a dramatic turn.

It was Christmas Day of that year when fate intervened. I was working one-on-one with a kidney transplant patient when I saw the helicopter touch down outside the hospital. The sight of it mesmerized me. One of the crew members was someone I knew, Benny Scott. Later that day, as I was leaving the building, I found Benny sitting on a bench, waiting for his wife to finish her shift. Something compelled me to ask him, "Do you ever use a nurse on that thing?" He admitted he wasn't sure, but he promised to find out. Little did I know that one of the EMTs had just dropped out, creating an opening.

A few days later, Dr. Tom Zirkle, the program's visionary medical leader, interviewed me by the staff elevators. Then, in January, I had a phone interview with Norm Meyer, the administrator. By February, I was flying.

Dr Tom Zirkle

Norm Meyer

Photo Credits: Loma Linda Digital Archives

One of my most memorable flights was a late-night mission to Brawley. A patient with severe cardiac issues needed to be transported to Daniel Freeman Hospital in Los Angeles.

His EKG was alarming, and his wife was understandably distraught. I took a moment to comfort her, holding her hand and reassuring her that we would do everything we could. As we lifted off, the patient's heart rhythm stabilized into a normal sinus rhythm, remaining steady throughout the flight. When we arrived, I handed over the EKG strip to the nurse in the CCU. Just as I finished my report, the patient's heart rhythm deteriorated again. It was a stark reminder of how fragile life can be.

Months later, I ran into the patient's neighbor at my bank. She recognized me from the flight and told me he had undergone a quadruple bypass and was doing well. Hearing that news was deeply satisfying. It reinforced why we took on such a challenging and often perilous job.

Our team was small but mighty. Benny Scott, Malcolm—whose last name escapes me—and the volunteer EMTs who formed the initial crew were all extraordinary individuals. The program itself was the brainchild of Alex Ferguson of Western Helicopters, who partnered with Dr. Zirkle to make it a reality. At the time, there was no precedent for what we were doing. We were breaking new ground with every flight.

The camaraderie among the crew was one of the best parts of the job. We were like family. We celebrated victories together and mourned losses deeply. I'll never forget September 1976, when our first helicopter crashed in the Cajon Pass. I'd been flying in that very ship all day before heading home. When I learned of the crash, my heart sank. Dick, our paramedic, had taken the call that evening. He didn't make it back. The loss was devastating, not only to our tight-knit team but to the entire hospital community.

Despite the risks, I continued flying until June 1977. By then, the program had evolved significantly. We added a second helicopter and even a fixed-wing aircraft to extend our reach. Our pilots were Vietnam veterans, seasoned and unflappable. They brought thousands of flight hours and an unshakable sense of duty to the program. One of our pilots, Gus Bliss, was particularly memorable. He later moved to Apache Junction, but his humor and skill left a lasting impression.

We encountered all kinds of challenges—weather being a frequent adversary. I remember one flight to March Air Force Base where we barely outran a wall of fog chasing us down the runway. The pilots' expertise in navigating such conditions was nothing short of miraculous.

One particularly unforgettable flight took us deep into the desert to retrieve a patient in critical condition. The desert's vast expanse and the isolation of the location added to the gravity of the mission. As we landed, the sheer silence of the desert was broken only by the roar of the helicopter blades. The patient was barely clinging to life, and every second counted. The intense heat made it feel like we were working in an oven, but we managed to stabilize the patient and bring him back to Loma Linda. Missions like these underscored the importance of the program and the impact it had on remote communities.

Another vivid memory is of a flight to Lone Pine, a small town nestled in the Sierra Nevada foothills. The patient, a middle-aged man, was experiencing severe cardiac distress. As we prepared for takeoff, his condition worsened, with premature ventricular contractions occurring more frequently. Knowing we couldn't wait, I requested a dose of lidocaine from the pilot, who relayed the request to the ground crew. Administering the medication stabilized the patient long enough for us to reach our destination. Looking out of the helicopter window during that flight, I was struck by the beauty of the snow-covered mountains, a stark contrast to the life-or-death struggle unfolding inside the cabin.

We often transported multiple patients at once, especially during emergencies. I remember one particularly grueling flight where we carried four patients simultaneously. As the only medical personnel on board, the responsibility was overwhelming. The confined space of the helicopter made every movement deliberate and precise. By the time we landed, I was physically and emotionally drained. After that flight, I vowed never to undertake such a task alone again.

The program's impact was immense. We transported patients from remote areas who otherwise wouldn't have survived. We were the bridge between life and death for so many. And though I often didn't know the outcomes of the patients we transported, the moments when I did—like the man from Brawley—made it all worthwhile.

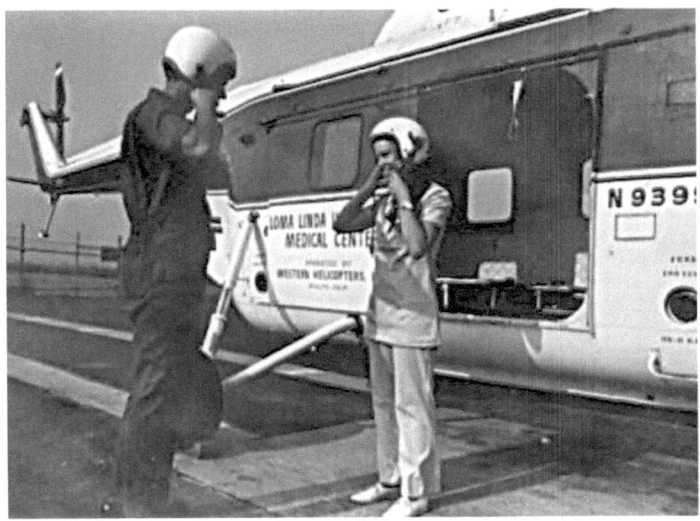

Photo Credit: Dawn Graves

In those days, our medical equipment was rudimentary compared to today's standards. We had a monitor, a defibrillator, and basic supplies. Contrast that with the advanced setups in modern medevac helicopters, which are essentially flying emergency rooms. Still, we made do with what we had and saved countless lives in the process.

The helicopter program at Loma Linda set the stage for similar initiatives across the country. St. Anthony's Hospital in Denver launched their program just a few months after ours, and the concept quickly gained traction nationwide. We were part of something much bigger than ourselves—a revolution in emergency medicine.

After I left the program, I stayed in nursing for several more years, exploring different roles from home care to teaching. Each position brought its own set of challenges and rewards, but nothing quite matched the adrenaline and fulfillment of those helicopter flights.

Even now, decades later, I find myself reminiscing about those days. I think about the patients, the flights, and the incredible team that made it all possible. I think about the lessons I learned and the lives we touched. And I think about the legacy we created at Loma Linda—a legacy that continues to save lives and inspire others to this day.

Reflecting further, it's remarkable to consider the global influence of programs like ours. Helicopter-based emergency services have since become standard practice worldwide, and it's humbling to know that we helped pave the way. I often wonder how Dr. Zirkle envisioned the future when he and Alex Ferguson took that leap of faith to establish the program. Their courage and innovation have saved countless lives over the decades, proving that bold ideas can lead to extraordinary outcomes.

The friendships I forged during those years have also stayed with me. Though time and distance have separated us, the bond we shared remains unbroken. We were a family, united by a common purpose and a willingness to take risks for the greater good. Whether it was celebrating milestones or comforting each other during tragedies, we faced it all together. It's a testament to the strength of the human spirit and the power of teamwork.

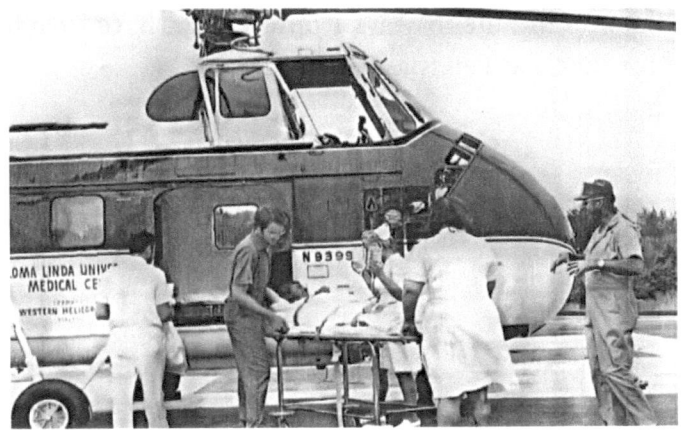

Photo Credit: Dawn Graves

One of the most touching moments came years later when I visited Loma Linda for a reunion. Standing on the helipad of the new hospital, I couldn't help but marvel at how far the program had come. The modern facilities and state-of-the-art helicopters were a far cry from our humble beginnings, but the mission remained the same: saving lives.

As I watched a helicopter lift off that day, memories of my first flight came rushing back. I thought about Benny, Dr. Zirkle, and all the other pioneers who made it possible. I thought about the patients whose lives were forever changed because we answered the call. And I thought about the future, knowing that the seeds we planted in those early days would continue to grow and flourish for generations to come.

Being part of Loma Linda's helicopter program was more than just a job; it was a calling. It taught me the value of resilience, the importance of innovation, and the power of compassion. Those lessons have stayed with me throughout my life, guiding me in ways I never could have imagined. And for that, I am eternally grateful.

Chapter 2

First National Bank of Loma Linda.

Photo Credit: Loma Linda Digital Archives

On an ill-fated morning, three would-be bandits, Walter Barrat, Anthony Maddox, and Robert Burbouski, concocted a plan that promised an easy payday but quickly turned into an elaborate comedy of errors. Their target was an former bank in Loma Linda, only to discover, in a twist of cosmic irony, that the bank had recently been sold and was no longer in operation. Undeterred, the trio pressed on, hoping there might still be some money stashed within.

As they entered, Mrs. R. L. Atcheson, working quietly at her desk, glanced up. "Get me the money," Burbouski ordered, brandishing his gun. Unfazed, Mrs. Atcheson simply replied, "There is no money here; this isn't a bank anymore." Just then, Irvin D. Lane, an insurance agent in the building, emerged from his office, adding to the chaotic scene. Trying to salvage their failed heist, the bandits redirected their focus to him, ordering him toward the vault.

Halfway to the vault, fate intervened in the form of a heroic watchmaker named G. W. Brown. Seeing the commotion from his mezzanine workshop, Brown seized a pair of shiny pliers, raised them as if they were a firearm, and shouted, "Come on, get out of here, or I'll start shooting!" The bandits froze, momentarily tricked by Brown's bold bluster and his "weapon." Even Lane, unsure whether Brown had an actual gun, marveled at the surprising turn of events.

Photo Credit: Loma Linda Digital Archives

Hustling out in a panic, the gang piled into their gray Chevrolet coupe, license plates hastily swapped with stolen ones to throw off any potential pursuers. However, in their haste, they'd barely hit the road before a fireworks stand attendant noticed them tear around the corner on two wheels, marking their escape route.

Their luck continued to plummet. After a quick pit stop at a service station near Highland to refuel and attempt another robbery, the bandits found themselves under the watchful eyes of Deputy Sheriff B. W. Brown and State Traffic Officers Otis Custer and Winston in Victorville. Following the crooks out of town to avoid a public showdown, the officers made their move, pulling the car over and swiftly arresting the trio without any further fuss.

In the end, the bandits' journey was nothing but a bumbling tour through mishap after mishap. Their grand heist was thwarted by a watchmaker with a pair of pliers, their getaway hampered by a haphazard route through Redlands, and their final attempt at escape stymied by officers who saw through their ill-conceived plan.

Photo Credit: Loma Linda Digital Archives

Chapter 3

Dr. Leonard Bailey

There is no way I could write a book about Loma Linda and not mention Dr. Leonard Bailey, who had one of the biggest impacts in my life of anyone.

Shortly after the headlines around Baby Faye filled television screens across the nation, my own daughter was born. Because I was self-employed at the time and did not have health insurance, my wife and I searched for the most affordable option and chose San Bernardino Community Hospital. That is where she came into the world. For a few days everything seemed normal, but less than a week later we began to notice troubling signs. Our baby was weak, lethargic, and simply not thriving. The feeling in our home shifted quickly from joy to dread. Parents know instinctively when something is wrong, and we could tell it was serious.

We were referred to a cardiologist in San Bernardino, Dr. Hunter Crittenden. I can still picture the examination room where he looked over our newborn. He was calm and professional, but after only a short time he gave us a verdict that turned our world upside down: "Your daughter is in heart failure." He said it plainly, without theatrics, but the words dropped like a thunderclap. In that moment, it felt like the walls closed in. I remember leaving the office dazed, as though I was in someone else's nightmare. The joy of a new life suddenly collided with the reality that without surgery she would not survive.

Our resources were limited, and the clock was ticking. I did the only thing I could: reached out to the people who had always been there for me. My grandmother had worked more than thirty years at St. Bernardine's Hospital in San Bernardino, where she became fast friends with the nuns. On her days off she would load her Volkswagen van with sisters in their habits and drive them to the beach, to Palm Springs, or to Knott's Berry Farm. They laughed together and shared adventures, and over time she called them her very best friends. Those friendships, built over decades, would soon prove to be a lifeline.

My family doctor, Jim Whitlock, was the other person I turned to. He was the kind of physician who could have stepped right out of a Norman Rockwell painting—thoughtful, gentle, always with a reassuring word. When I explained what had happened, he did not dismiss me or tell me to wait. Instead he said, "Let me work on it. I've got some ideas." I didn't know what he meant, but the fact that he was already thinking of solutions steadied me.

As it turned out, both my grandmother and Dr. Whitlock went to work immediately in ways that could only be described as providential. My grandmother called her closest friend among the sisters, Sister Mary Lambert, who by then was retired and living in Texas. "Let me see what I can do," Sister Lambert told her. Meanwhile, Jim Whitlock picked up the phone and called one of his longtime colleagues and friends, a name that had been on every newscast in America in those weeks: Dr. Leonard Bailey. To my astonishment, Jim called me back the very same day. "I just spoke to Leonard," he said. "He's agreed to do the surgery as a favor."

That left us nearly speechless. This was the same Dr. Bailey who had been on television, the man at the center of international headlines, who was pioneering surgeries no one had dared attempt. We could not believe that someone of his caliber would consider helping us, an ordinary family with no connections and no insurance.

The next call came from Sister Lambert. She had used her influence to speak with the leadership at St. Bernardine's. "You're taken care of," she told my grandmother. "The operation can be done there, and everything will be covered. You don't need to worry about a thing."

There remained one practical obstacle: Dr. Bailey did not have staff privileges at St. Bernardine's. That alone might have stopped the process in its tracks. But Sister Lambert, with her persistence and the weight of her reputation, managed to convince the administrator to grant Dr. Bailey temporary privileges so he could perform the operation. Looking back, I remain amazed at how doors opened in just the right sequence.

I will never forget meeting Dr. Bailey in person. From the way the news media covered him, one might have expected a man larger than life, commanding and perhaps even distant. Instead, he was one of the most soft-spoken, gentle, and kind individuals I have ever encountered. He greeted us quietly, explained what needed to be done, and gave us a sense of calm that cut through the chaos. In his presence, the overwhelming burden we carried lifted just enough for us to breathe.

The surgery went forward at St. Bernardine's. The nuns went so far as to provide my wife a hospital room so she could remain near our daughter throughout the ordeal. That simple act of kindness spoke volumes about the culture of compassion in which Dr. Bailey worked. The procedure was successful. Days later, we began to see color in our baby's cheeks, the strength returning to her small body. Nearly forty years have passed since that day, and our daughter has never again had a cardiac problem. That one surgery appears to have restored her heart for life.

To say that Dr. Bailey changed our lives is an understatement. He gave our daughter a future and gave us the chance to raise her, watch her grow, and enjoy the simple blessings of family that so many take for granted. To us he was not simply a world-famous surgeon—he was a man who cared, who listened, who treated us with dignity when we had nothing to offer in return.

Leonard L. Bailey came to Loma Linda in 1965 with a single dream: to become a heart surgeon. He graduated from the School of Medicine in 1969 and went to Toronto for residency training at the Hospital for Sick Children, where he specialized in pediatric cardiac surgery. His focus soon narrowed to the tiniest and most fragile patients—newborns with congenital heart defects. The condition that haunted him most was hypoplastic left-heart syndrome, a lethal underdevelopment of the left side of the heart. Perfectly healthy babies in every other respect would die within days because their small hearts could not pump blood effectively. For Bailey, watching these infants slip away was intolerable.

He pursued answers relentlessly. By the early 1980s, he had concluded that heart transplantation offered the best chance. In October 1984, he attempted what the world then considered impossible: transplanting the heart of a baboon into a newborn girl later known to the public as Baby Fae. The operation transfixed the globe. Newspapers splashed it across front pages, television stations broadcast updates daily, and debates raged in classrooms, pulpits, and legislative chambers. Baby Fae lived twenty-one days before her tiny body rejected the organ. Though the outcome was heartbreaking, the procedure marked a turning point. It demonstrated that infant transplantation could be attempted, and with refinements, could succeed.

Few know that behind the scenes, two baboons had been readied in the animal care facility as potential donors. Staff nicknamed them Raisinette and Goobers. Raisinette provided the heart used in the surgery. The very existence of such details underscored just how experimental those early days were, and how Bailey pushed forward into uncharted territory because he could not bear to watch babies die without trying.

For Dr. Bailey, the story was never about medical headlines or professional glory. He often spoke about the deeper motivation that guided him. "Few life events on earth exceed the realization of love, the miracle of conception, or the emotion of birthing," he wrote. "Babies are naturally embraced by hope... unless the heart within a baby's breast is so poorly developed that life cannot go on. I have been driven by the notion that heart disease should not end the promise of a newborn infant." He confessed that he was "a real patsy when it comes to looking into a baby's eyes and dreaming about the potential for this little person."

Those were not empty words. Colleagues recalled that he spent long hours at the bedside of his young patients, not just in the operating room but in the quiet moments afterward, checking on them, speaking gently to anxious parents, and making sure families knew he was in their corner. He once remarked that saving babies made a statement about humanity itself: "We need babies. We need the statement that saving babies makes."

The world may remember him most for Baby Fae, but his larger legacy was the hundreds of successful infant heart transplants that followed. The once-unimaginable became standard practice. Over the years Bailey and his team performed more than three hundred such operations. Many of those children grew to adulthood, some even became parents themselves, living out futures that would never have existed had he not taken that first step.

Of course, the road was not easy. Bailey endured protests from animal rights activists, criticism from ethicists, and the immense pressure of the international media spotlight. Yet those who knew him best said that none of that changed his steady demeanor. He remained the same man I encountered at St. Bernardine's—soft-spoken, humble, and caring.

In 2002, at a celebration honoring the eighty-seventh birthday of his colleague Dr. Ellsworth Wareham, Bailey offered words that revealed the spiritual depth behind his work: "We have had the opportunity as medical professionals to actually live the talk and live the life that God intended. That's what we're planted on Earth for. I thank you so much for the time we've spent together."

That was the essence of Leonard Bailey. He believed his calling was not only scientific but spiritual—that saving babies was part of God's plan for his life and the lives of his colleagues. He lived that calling fully.

For my family, he will always be the man who gave our daughter her life back. For countless others, he was the surgeon who transformed despair into hope. His legacy cannot be measured only in medical advances, or even in the hundreds of successful operations, but in the quiet gratitude of parents who tucked their children into bed at night because of him.

Leonard Bailey not only made medical history. He gave the gift of a future.

Chapter 4

Elder Wayne White

As I reflect on my Loma Linda neighborhood and the people who shaped my early years, I would be remiss not to mention a dear friend and mentor of mine, Wayne W. White. Wayne was a retired minister, but his influence on me was more rooted in business than in spirituality. Few may remember him today, but his impact on me, and many LLU graduate students, was profound.

When Wayne retired from ministry, he dedicated himself to providing affordable housing for as many LLU graduate students as possible. The house in the picture is a prime example of his approach. You might wonder why a house like this has so many parking spaces—there was a reason.

Wayne would buy affordable homes, often those displaced by the crosstown freeway project, for less than $1,000. (The one in the photo is a prime example.) He'd then hire a house-moving company to transport them to a vacant lot and transform them into duplexes, triplexes, or even quadruplexes. He did it as economically as possible. He hired me to do the electrical work, even though I was just a teenage, unlicensed electrician at the time. I had learned the trade from a young age, and Wayne liked my main qualification: I worked very cheaply. I remember converting laundry rooms into kitchens and closets into bathrooms more times than I could count.

Another trick I learned from him was to make friends with a cabinet shop. We had a mutual friend who specialized in remodeling kitchens. I remember a couple of times when I went with Wayne (remember, I worked cheap), and together, we carefully removed old cabinets, countertops, and sinks from remodel projects. Wayne taught me how to laminate Formica to plywood, a skill that saved us a fortune. He knew where to buy sheets with slight defects at a fraction of the cost. We'd make new countertops, repaint the old cabinets, and presto—a (almost) free kitchen unit.

I marveled at how he could take an average-sized house and reconfigure it into three or four small apartments. Wayne also taught me where to find the best bargains on materials and furnishings. His main supplier was Presco in San Bernardino, a place specializing in used materials. There was another spot in Rubidoux called Rolling Hills Auction, where we bought carpet for $1 a yard and paint for 50 cents a gallon. I'd often accompany him down to Orange County to a fiberglass manufacturing facility, where we could buy damaged or blemished shower enclosures and vanities for as little as $2 each. He even taught me how to repair fiberglass.

Another way Wayne saved money was by skipping permits. When inspectors occasionally showed up, he would put an arm around their shoulders and explain how the medical students living in these apartments would go on to save thousands of lives. Wayne was a charming man, and for some reason, he always reminded me of Floyd the Barber from The Andy Griffith Show.

At that time, student loans were scarce, and many students worked part-time while their spouses worked full-time to make ends meet. Most were very poor. Wayne not only offered them affordable rent but would often let them work off part of their rent by painting, cleaning, and doing yard work at his rental properties.

I eventually adopted many of Wayne's practices, transforming houses into small apartments and using his suppliers. There was one thing, however, I couldn't bring myself to copy: I always took out permits. I just didn't have Wayne's knack for charming my way out of those with inspectors.

Chapter 5

Ritchie Mansion

I was aware of the Ritchie Mansion since I was a little kid. I just never knew the story behind it until a classmate, Jane Ritchie, gave me a brief explanation of its beginnings. Later, when I was undergoing proton treatment, I was offered the use of it for a very modest sum. I never sat down for a long interview about the house; beyond that first, short explanation, I pieced the rest together from what I could find—old notes, historical blurbs, and the kind of local details you pick up living here.

For years the place was background scenery for me—the big Victorian on the bend, half in the trees, the one you glimpse when you take the long way around campus. Once I started digging, the outline came into focus. The house rose in 1895, when the valley was still deciding what it wanted to be. Colonel J. T. Ritchie built it with care: woodwork that catches the light, a lively roofline, rooms enough to hold a large family and then some. It was built for a retired sea captain, Lewis S. Davis, who gave it a name that still feels right: Snug Harbor. That name reads like a promise—safe water after rough seas.

The Ritchie name came later, when the family bought the place and folded it into their story. That's how most of us learned it, growing up: the Ritchie Mansion. By the time I was old enough to remember street names, the house already felt like part of the neighborhood's voice. I rode past it on bikes and in cars without knowing anything more than how it looked in afternoon light.

What I didn't recognize then is how closely the house would end up tied to Loma Linda's mission. In the mid-1990s, the university brought the property into the fold. A practical renovation followed in the early 2000s—one that respected what the old house was while making it useful for what people needed now. The grand rooms that once held big gatherings were shaped into smaller living spaces: seven simple studios where someone could sleep, make a meal, and, most importantly, walk to their appointments.

If you've never stayed there, picture a day in small, ordinary notes. Morning comes with gentle sounds: a door closed carefully, a kettle, the soft shuffle of someone checking a schedule before heading out. Around midday there might be a face on the porch with a paperback, or a phone call to family back home. Evenings, the lamps warm up behind the windows and the house settles into a steady, familiar rhythm. Nobody is trying to impress anybody. The house is doing its job.

A modern building might beat it on square footage or uniformity, but it can't offer the same kind of reassurance. Old places that have lasted send a quiet message without words: you're part of a longer story. Others have been here and got through their hard season. When you're measuring progress by inches and counting days, that message matters. It's another kind of medicine, delivered by porch steps and floorboards.

The story line is simple once you see it: a sea captain created a haven; a builder made it sturdy enough to last; a family kept it alive; a university recognized its potential and put it back to work. Not every landmark gets that kind of second life. Many become museum pieces, nice to look at and easy to ignore. This one stayed useful by changing its job—still a harbor, just for a different kind of voyage.

I was grateful for that on a personal level. When I was offered a place there during proton therapy, what struck me wasn't only the modest cost, though that mattered. It was the feeling that someone had thought through the quiet parts of healing. The walk shouldn't be far. The kitchen should be easy. The chair should fit. The other tenants shouldn't be strangers for long. You find a new routine alongside the science: which tree throws afternoon shade, what time the breeze cools the porch, the short path toward the clinic. Ordinary anchors help when everything else is unusual.

There's a kind of craftsmanship in the way the house was updated. New wiring threads through stubborn walls, plumbing learns new routes, and partitions create private spaces without erasing what gives the place its character. Keep the bones, add the arteries. That blend of old and new feels like Loma Linda to me. We're a town that prefers "and" over "or."

I've walked that block at different times and the house has a way of meeting the moment. Morning is clean light and hopeful footsteps. Afternoon is a pause in the shade. Evening is the soft hum of a building that knows how to hold still for people. If a place can hold its breath for you, this one does.

Some folks ask why keep a Victorian at all. Why not put up a modern box and standardize everything? There's an answer in the faces of the people coming and going. A place with history lends you some of its steadiness. It reminds you that the town didn't spring up yesterday and won't disappear tomorrow. That context can be worth as much as the view from a window. It says: take your time, you've got a roof that's looked after a lot of lives.

Every now and then I stop on the sidewalk and look up at the eaves. The house has seen horse-drawn days, quiet groves, new roads, campus buildings rising, hospital lights at night, and now a line of people who come for a kind of treatment nobody imagined when those boards were first cut. It has carried all that without turning precious. It stays useful. The seven studios aren't fancy. They're enough. Enough is a comfort when you're living appointment to appointment. A chair that feels familiar after the second day, a short walk to where you need to be, a front door you can find in your sleep—that's the promise the mansion keeps.

The name still fits because of what happens inside. A harbor doesn't fix the ship; it gives the ship a calm place to be repaired. The real work happens with the crew and the tools, but none of it matters without a place to anchor. That's what this old house does for people in treatment. You turn a key, step into a room that belongs to you for a while, and your legs steady. You set the folder down, make toast, sit, and become a person again instead of a case number. That's a small miracle in the middle of bigger ones.

When I pass it now, I see more than a handsome survivor. I see history pressed into service, generosity expressed in square footage, and a reminder of what this town values: comfort and dignity alongside technology. It's a landmark that keeps working, which might be the best kind of landmark a place like Loma Linda can have.

I was aware of the Ritchie Mansion since I was a little kid. I learned its beginnings in a few short lines. The rest I collected the way people collect the past here—patiently, from what's left behind. And I learned, when I needed it most, what it means for a community to offer a safe place close by. That's how I remember the house on the bend: steady, useful, and still doing the quiet work Loma Linda is known for.

Chapter 6

Loma Linda Chocolate Prune Cake-Recipe and Stories

By Robert Peterson.

The Chocolate Prune Cake Vendetta.

It was a typical day at the bakery, where everything ran like clockwork—until it didn't. Steve, the man in charge of making the famous chocolate-filled prune cake, was overseeing the batter with his usual no-nonsense attitude. This cake was a specialty, and its ingredients list was unique: batter, chocolate, and finely ground prunes. Steve had his own method for prepping the prunes, even if it wasn't exactly by the book.

Instead of using the tamping stick to push the prunes into the electric grinder, he opted for his hand—a shortcut he'd taken before. I was just a teenager, a "flunky," as they'd say, tasked with washing pots and pans. Steve, on the other hand, was the seasoned baker, a guy everyone respected. That's probably why I didn't think twice about hearing him mutter about getting the job done faster.

Suddenly, a scream pierced the air. I whipped around and saw him stumble back, clutching his hand, his face pale. Blood arced across the wall as he yanked his hand from the grinder—three fingers were missing, ground into the batter. It was a horror I'd never imagined seeing in that bakery, and a sickening silence settled as he was bundled off to the ER.

Then came the directive: "Don't waste the batter," the boss muttered, barely looking my way. My new job? Picking out the "big chunks" of Steve's fingers from the five-gallon vat of batter. It was an unforgettable moment, and as I grimly scooped out what I could, one thought wouldn't leave my mind:

"That's the day Steve put a little bit of himself into that cake."

On a lighter chocolate prune cake–related note, working nights at the bakery was my first real job, and I owed it to Fred, the manager of the market—and my neighbor. Fred had hired me the moment I turned fourteen, maybe because he knew I could use a steady job or maybe because he figured I wouldn't complain about the grunt work. Either way, I was grateful, even if it meant spending most nights scrubbing down flour-caked counters and keeping the place spotless for the skilled bakers who'd arrive in the morning.

Chief among them was Art, the head baker. He was a serious guy, always arriving exactly at six in his crisp whites with his spotless baker's hat, which he'd place on his head with an exaggerated flourish. Art was practically a legend around the bakery. Rumor had it that he was the one who'd created the bakery's prized chocolate prune cake—a recipe he guarded closely, and which people swore only he knew by heart.

One night, around three a.m., I had a flash of inspiration. I grabbed Art's pristine white hat, dipped it in water, and stuck it in the freezer. When I saw his car pull up, I quickly retrieved the frosty hat and set it back on the shelf. Right on cue, Art strolled in, ready to bake his famous cake. He went through his usual routine, grabbed his hat, and—with his signature flair—set it on his head. The second the frozen hat touched his scalp, he froze, then went wide-eyed with outrage as an icy chill spread across his head. He looked around and locked onto me.

"Why me?" I shrugged, trying to keep a straight face. "There are other people here, you know."

Art wasn't buying it. Not long after, Fred called me into his office. He was holding back a smirk. "Did you freeze Art's hat?" he asked.

I couldn't lie to Fred. After all, he was my neighbor, and I didn't want to jeopardize the job he'd given me. I admitted to it, bracing for a lecture.

Instead, Fred chuckled. "Alright, don't do it again."

And that was the morning I'd managed to prank the creator of the famous chocolate prune cake. Art may have been a legend, but at least for one chilly moment, I had the last laugh.

Ingredients:

- ¼ cup boiling water
- ¾–1 cup pitted prunes
- ¾ cup oil
- 1 cup sugar
- 2 tablespoons cocoa
- 2 teaspoons cinnamon
- 1 teaspoon salt
- 1 teaspoon vanilla
- 2 eggs
- ¾ cup buttermilk
- 2¼ cups flour

- ½ teaspoon baking soda
- 2 teaspoons baking powder

Chocolate Fudge Icing:

- ¼ cup water
- ¼ cup shortening
- ¼ cup light corn syrup
- 2 cups sifted confectioners sugar
- ⅛ cup cocoa
- ¼ teaspoon salt
- ½ teaspoon vanilla

Cake:

1. Pour boiling water over prunes and let soak 30 minutes.

2. Combine oil, sugar, cocoa, cinnamon, salt, and vanilla in bowl. Add eggs and beat well for two minutes.

3. Combine soaked prunes and buttermilk in blender container or food processor bowl and chop finely.

4. Add prune mixture with flour, baking soda, and baking powder. Beat well and turn into well-greased and floured 13x9-inch baking pan or

two 8-inch round pans.

5. Bake at 350 degrees for 30 minutes, or until a wooden toothpick inserted near center comes out clean.

6. Cool and frost with Chocolate Fudge Icing.

Icing:

1. Bring water to a boil. Remove from heat and beat in shortening and corn syrup.

2. Add sifted sugar, cocoa, salt, and vanilla gradually. Beat until smooth and creamy. Ice will spread when slightly warm

Chapter 7

Phil the Plumber

(At Least He Wasn't an Electrician)

I first knew Phil Quishenberry when I was just a kid. Two things always stood out about him. One, he could make me laugh every time we talked. Two, he had a trick no one else I ever met could do: he could touch the top of a door and the floor at the same time. Try it — it's impossible, unless you were Phil. The last time I saw him, about five years ago, both his humor and his knack for surprising people were still very much alive.

Phil was born June 26, 1937, at six o'clock on a Sabbath morning in Ketchum, Oklahoma, the seventh of Thomas and Evelyn Quishenberry's children. His birth came during the hardships of the Great Depression. Only a year before, tragedy had struck when the family's oldest son, Roy, was killed by lightning at the age of seventeen. Phil's arrival was a balm in that grief, and Evelyn always said his birth helped heal her heart.

The Quishenberry family knew what it meant to struggle. They tried moving to Idaho, but soon found themselves in trouble when some of the older children started getting into mischief. They returned to Oklahoma with nowhere to live, so friends offered them a tent by a stream. To the neighborhood children, it looked like camping, with swimming and play at the water's edge. But when winter closed in, survival was another matter. Another neighbor offered an unused chicken house, and the family moved in, using cardboard partitions to make "rooms." These were Depression years, when nearly everyone was poor, scraping by with whatever work they could find.

Phil's earliest years were filled with chores. One Sabbath morning when he was three, his family discovered he was missing. A search party formed, only to see the family cows coming home by themselves — being driven along by little Phil in diapers, waving a stick. Later, while living in a labor camp in Washington's Yakima Valley, he was responsible for hauling trash, cleaning bathrooms, and milking the family cow before school.

His stories from those days always carried humor. He loved telling how, while cleaning women's bathrooms, the women would keep using the stalls. They'd just lift their feet so he could sweep underneath. Sometimes, unable to resist, Phil tossed ice water over the stall doors, sending squeals through the building. He would laugh for years telling that one, and everyone who knew him marveled that he survived childhood with a sense of humor intact.

Even in discipline, Phil managed to turn the tables. Once, at dinner, his father became angry and told him to fetch a switch. Phil returned with a flimsy twig. Ordered to get a larger one, he came back with a slightly bigger but still useless stick. Furious now, his father barked, "Don't come back until you bring a real switch." Phil disappeared and returned dragging a massive branch, heavy enough to flatten him if it had ever been used. His siblings burst out laughing, his father broke down in laughter too, and Phil escaped punishment entirely. It was the only time he ever managed to talk himself out of a whipping, and it became part of family legend.

By high school, Phil was earning his own money, buying clothes, paying tuition at the Adventist school, and working orchard jobs. His picking skills became the stuff of legend. In one season, while the standard wage was a dollar an hour, Phil picked 358 boxes of apples in a single day. At 42 pounds each, that came to more than seven tons of fruit — 15,000 pounds — in twelve hours. He earned $71.60 that day, what would have been a full week's wages for most men.

A turning point came when his sister Georgia and her husband George Randolph invited Phil to live with them in Loma Linda and attend Loma Linda Academy. From that moment on, Loma Linda became his permanent home. He thrived at the Academy, graduating in 1955 as student body president and athlete of the year. He helped George with construction projects, including working on the Loma Linda University Dental School. The memory of those warm

Southern California winters, compared to the cold of the Northwest, stuck with him. "I thought I had died and gone to heaven," he said, and he never left.

Phil's athletic ability was remarkable. He was a natural at softball and bowling. In fast-pitch softball, he threw near 100 miles per hour. His bat was just as dangerous. People still recall how he would hit balls clean out of the Redlands park, bouncing them across the street into the McDonald's parking lot. While serving as a medic in the U.S. Army, his unit was called to Vietnam even though he had less than a year left in service. The reason? His commanding officer loved baseball, and Phil was the team's pitcher. He set up the first field hospital in Vietnam, worked his shifts as a medic, then played ball. His family once spotted him on *Wide World of Sports* pitching in a military softball tournament.

Back in Loma Linda during the 1960s, he played on the Randolph Plumbing team, often facing Gay 90's Pizza. Gay 90's was a Redlands institution where everything was stapled to the walls — menus, receipts, and newspaper clippings. After one game, a headline read "Quishenberry Shuts Out Gay 90's." I couldn't resist circling his name and writing a note that Phil hated Gay 90's Pizza and loved Shakey's. Soon, the Randolph Plumbing shop got calls from angry Gay 90's fans. Neither Phil nor George found it funny, but I still do.

I spent three decades working alongside him — he as the plumber, me as the electrician. We had a running debate about which trade was smarter and better looking. It never got resolved. But it gave us endless banter and laughs through long days on construction sites. Once, eating lunch under a tree at a house in San Bernardino, we talked about how we wanted to be remembered. Phil smiled and said, "At least I wasn't an electrician." It was the perfect Quishenberry punchline — delivered with a straight face, but leaving everyone laughing.

Phil's working life shaped Loma Linda in ways people may not realize. He laid pipe in the old hospital towers, worked on expansions at the university, and built infrastructure in countless homes across the valley. He was everywhere. His little blue Toyota truck was a familiar sight in town, seeming almost comically small for his large frame. Customers said that when Phil showed up, you got more than plumbing. One remembered, "I loved Phil. He could fix your faucet, update you on the community gossip, give child-rearing tips, and share the love of Jesus — all for one price."

In 1964, Phil married the love of his life. Six days before their wedding, a butane gas explosion at the Calimesa church burned his face, neck, and arm. He was hospitalized with second- and third-degree burns but persuaded doctors to let him go. He drove overnight to Oregon for the ceremony, shaving off scabs so his bride wouldn't see them, and they married as planned. They honeymooned in Hawaii, bandaging his wounds daily. For the next 58 years, Phil never stopped bragging about her — her talents, her intelligence, her cooking.

Together, they raised two sons, Tom and Mike, in their Loma Linda home. Phil worked sixty-hour weeks, yet he still washed cars every Friday for Sabbath, played catch with the boys, and took family trips to Joshua Tree. Later, as a grandfather, he poured himself into Bailey, Jamie, Kiko, Drew, and Shawnee. He called time with them "a slice of heaven."

Phil finally retired in his seventies when neuropathy made it impossible to carry his 90-pound toolbox. Even then, he stayed cheerful, reading the paper, watching baseball, and doing daily word searches with his wife. When he passed peacefully in 2022, his sons summed him up perfectly: in heaven, Phil will be hitting home runs over the sea of glass, telling jokes to the disciples, and still debating whether plumbers or electricians are smarter.

For me, the image is simpler. I picture him with that grin, making me laugh, or touching the top of a door and the floor at the same time — an impossible trick, unless you were Phil. He left Loma Linda stronger, funnier, and warmer than he found it. And my own life was better for knowing him.

Chapter 8

The Granary

It Seemed Like a Good Idea

I was in my twenties when the sign for the Granary went up at Tippecanoe and Redlands Boulevard, on the site where Nelson Plumbing had been. A vegetarian restaurant fit Loma Linda, where healthy living was already a community habit.

The Granary was started by John Pelt—Elder Pelt to many of us—my former pastor from the Redlands Church. The purpose was clear: simple, good food aligned with local values. The room was straightforward and uncluttered.

Two newspaper ads captured both the creativity and the tension in the concept. They promoted an "un-burger," a playful echo of 7Up's "Un-cola," and in places paired it with Coke. The messaging also made room for a meat option.

Those choices sent mixed signals: the branding leaned toward health and a vegetarian identity, while the menu and pairings reached for conventional fast-food expectations.

Operationally, the mixed signals showed up on the grill. Offering meat meant cooking it on the same surface as the vegetarian items, which turned away many who kept a strict vegetarian kitchen. Closing on Saturday added another challenge. It meant the restaurant missed one of the strongest traffic windows for out-of-home dining, as industry data commonly shows weekends—often Friday and Saturday—among the busiest days of the week for restaurants.

The drive-thru was a smart decision for the corner, but the layout worked against it. Because the building sat at a 45-degree angle, the lane forced a sharp, almost U-turn. In larger vehicles you could find yourself backing up, pulling forward, backing up again, and still climbing a curb on the way out.

There's a business adage worth remembering: you can't please everybody all the time; at best you please most of the people half the time—or half the people most of the time. In hindsight, that seems like the line the Granary straddled. By trying to welcome everyone, they ended up with a double barrier: meat-eaters hesitant to be seen at a place that appeared vegetarian, and vegetarians hesitant to eat where meat shared the grill and fries and soda felt like the default sides.

A different path might have strengthened the idea they started with: lean fully into the health-food identity that already had an audience in town—more like the Patio Pantry or the campus diner—center the menu on hearty salads, whole-grain plates, and distinctive vegetable wraps, and let the un-burger be a true flagship.

The arc of that corner is simple after that. The Granary's run ended; the site became Naugles; later, after the brands merged, it turned into a Del Taco. If you drive by there today, that's what you'll find.

What remains is the intention and the lesson. The Granary carried a hopeful idea: that a restaurant in Loma Linda could reflect the best of the community's habits. The lesson is just as clear: a good plan gets stronger when the identity is consistent, from the ad to the grill. Even with its short life, the Granary mattered. It showed, in plain terms, what this town values—health, simplicity, and care—and it left a blueprint for how a concept like that can succeed by staying true to itself.

Chapter 9

Milton Corwin

It has been nearly sixty years since I first met Milton Corwin, and there are moments when it still feels like yesterday. That first encounter didn't come with any fanfare or warning. It was one of those quiet events that, at the time, seemed ordinary, but over the years became a permanent fixture in memory.

There was something about Milton—his presence, his words, his strength in the face of circumstances that would have broken most people—that left a lasting mark. He had a favorite expression: "Every day is Thanksgiving." At first it sounded simple, maybe even rehearsed. But it wasn't a slogan or something to fill silence. He meant it. He lived it. He radiated it. And once you spent any time around him, you couldn't help but begin seeing things a little differently yourself.

Milton had lived through more than most. Born in the late 1920s, he grew up on a farm outside Medford, Oregon. Life in that part of the country during those years was not easy. As a young man he worked as a lumberjack—back when that meant heavy axes, cold mornings, and the kind of grit that left little room for mistakes. The men who did it had to be part athlete, part soldier, and part mountain goat. Milton thrived in that world. He never backed down from the physical, the difficult, or even the dangerous. That toughness stayed with him throughout his life, but it was never arrogance. It was simply who he was: resilient, determined, self-reliant.

He liked to tell stories, sometimes with a dry humor that carried a hint of wisdom. One he shared was about being arrested as a teenager for littering. It wasn't quite the full-blown caper that Arlo Guthrie sang about years later, but it had a similar rhythm: a young man brushing against authority, learning something along the way.

And then came the war. When World War II broke out, Milton, like so many of his generation, did not hesitate. He served in Europe, where he faced things most of us could hardly imagine. He didn't talk much about those experiences, but you could sense the weight of them in the way he carried himself. He had seen the worst of what people could do to each other, and he came home determined to live better.

After the war he went to college in Nebraska. Always moving forward, always finding a way. But life does not always care about your plans. While he was still a student, Milton contracted polio. The illness struck quickly and left him a quadriplegic. For a time he lived in an iron lung, and later used one of the earliest electric wheelchairs, operating it with a joystick.

To most people, that would have been the end of the story—a promising young man suddenly cut down by a devastating disease. Milton saw it differently. If anything, it seemed to unlock something deeper. He told me once that he had never enjoyed life more than he did then. At the time I couldn't understand. But as I grew older, I realized what he meant. It wasn't that he enjoyed the limitations or the struggle. It was that he had learned to see what most of us miss: gratitude, clarity, perspective.

When Milton finished his studies, he moved to Loma Linda, California, where he built a full and active life. He lived in a small house behind his office, near the site of the new hospital. His business was simple but successful—selling insurance and real estate. He and his wife Bernice ran a money management company together called M&B Investments. They made a strong team.

But business was only part of his life. Milton was drawn toward service. He ran for city council when Loma Linda incorporated. He served as treasurer of the Pacific Outpost Foundation and directed Living Outreach, Inc., a nonprofit book ministry that distributed literature to motels, libraries, and storefronts. He was devoted to his church, and one of his proudest projects was helping to establish Oak

Glen Outpost, a center dedicated to natural remedies and healthful living. He believed in healing—not just the body, but the mind and spirit. He knew suffering, but he also knew what it meant to overcome.

The first time I saw Milton, I was about eight years old. I had never seen anyone in an iron lung before. To a child it looked frightening—loud, mechanical, and foreign. But the man inside it was the opposite. Milton smiled at me as if I were the only person in the room. He greeted me with a calm warmth that stayed with me.

He could only speak a few words at a time—each sentence required him to swallow air first—but when he spoke, you listened. His words carried weight. He wasn't dramatic, he didn't preach. He simply made you feel included, like he was inviting you to see the world in a better way.

Milton also had standards. I remember seeing him displeased once—not angry, but firm—when someone spoke unkindly about another person in his presence. He stopped it immediately. He believed in kindness, grace, and the goodness of people. He lived by those values, and he expected others around him to live by them as well.

Years later, when I watched the film Gandhi, I thought of Milton. The same quiet strength. The same refusal to let adversity become bitterness. The same relentless focus on what could be, rather than what had been lost.

Milton called his condition an "inconvenience." It was perhaps the most understated description I ever heard, but it revealed who he was. He wasn't interested in pity. He was interested in living fully. And he did.

He shaped his life into something meaningful—not in spite of his challenges, but because of them. Every day he reminded those around him that joy is possible, that gratitude is a choice, and that life is worth showing up for, even when it is hard.

Every Thanksgiving, I think of him. I remember his smile, his eyes lighting up with a story, the way he made everyone feel valued. I remember his words—"every day is Thanksgiving"—and I understand now what he meant. It was not about food or holidays. It was about seeing beauty in the everyday. About giving thanks for what you can do, not what you cannot. About recognizing that life, even when it knocks you down, also hands you unexpected moments of grace.

I don't always succeed, but I try to live that way too.

Milton died some years ago, but his influence lingers. I feel it in the way I handle setbacks, in the patience I try to practice, in the small joys I don't take for granted. He was one of the toughest men I ever met—not because of the muscles he once had as a lumberjack, or the battles he fought in Europe, but because of the way he faced life when it changed completely. He didn't flinch. He adapted. And he left behind a legacy that still ripples outward.

Milton Corwin taught me something I will never forget: gratitude does not depend on your circumstances—it defines them. Live with that kind of heart, and every day truly can be Thanksgiving.

Chapter 10
Hazels Beauty Bar
By: Margi Dalgleish Roth

Photo Credit: Margi Dalgleish Roth

In the fall of 1944, my mother was just 17, a junior at Loma Linda Academy. She was living at 24984 Barton Rd. with Ardis (Herman) and Art Robinson, charitable folks who gave her, an all-but-homeless teen, a place to live with familiar people, since her Uncle Henry had once been married to Mrs. Robinson's sister, Inez. Hazel Herman, the youngest sister of Ardis and Inez, owned a hair salon down on Anderson St., across from where the Campus Hill SDA Church now stands. Mom's father, who had left for good when she was just a toddler, helped build a house for the Herman family in the late 1920s, the house where Hazel lived alone in adulthood, between the train tracks and the wash on Van Leuven St. So these folks were like family to her.

Hazel's Beauty Bar

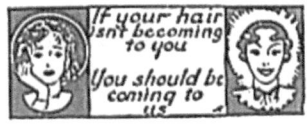

After school, my mom would often stop by Hazel's shop to visit as she walked home. It was a welcoming place to cool off, get a drink of cold water, and visit with Hazel and whoever might be in the salon chair. On one October day, Hazel was doing the hair of Verna Dalgleish, a friend of hers and, as it turned out, my dad's eldest sister. As they chatted, my mom mentioned that she wished she had a date for the weekend.

"What kind of guy are you looking for?" Hazel asked.

"Well, he should have a car and a job. And I'd like him to be tall, blond, and blue-eyed," Mom said, smiling.

Verna chimed in, "I have a 19-year-old younger brother who meets all of that—except he's not tall," she said. "But he's a good guy."

"Bring him on!" my mom replied, laughing.

A plan was made for them to meet at the young people's meeting at the Campus Hill Church in Loma Linda that Friday night. But fate had other ideas—Mom came down with chickenpox. Too sick to go out, she missed that first

Friday night. Then the next week came, and she still wasn't well enough. It took another week or two before she was finally able to go.

In the meantime, Dad kept going to the young people's meetings, looking for her, waiting to meet this mysterious girl. Finally, after three weeks or so, she was there. As Dad described it later, he saw her and said to himself, "That's the girl I'm going to marry!" They arranged their first date with the help of Art and Ardis, who were planning a trip up to Lake Arrowhead to go ice skating. Their courtship moved quickly. By Groundhog Day 1945, Dad was ready to pop the question. They drove to the Loma Linda Mound, a local landmark with a road looping around the top. Parked and overlooking the valley, he asked her to marry him. She said yes!

Ruthie and Milton Dalgleish

Photo Credit: Margi Dalgleish Roth

They were married on July 15, 1945, in the backyard of Art and Ardis Robinson's house, just a few steps away from where Hazel's Beauty Bar would eventually stand. Their wedding marked the beginning of what would become a 76-year love story. Mom passed away in 2021 at the age of 94, while Dad is still thriving at 99. We miss her every day.

By the time I was born in the late '50s, Hazel's shop had moved to its spot behind the garage of her sister's house on Barton Road. It even had a moving neon sign with a bell that would "ring" back and forth in neon blue, a nod to Hazel's middle name, Belle. That shop became a neighborhood fixture, its bell calling to mind the warm spirit and resilience that ran through the family.

As the years went by, Hazel remained a popular hairdresser among many of Loma Linda's elderly ladies. It was common for her to retrieve her no-longer-driving friends and clients, bring them to her shop to get their hair done, and drive them back home in her station wagon.

Hazel lived a full life, born on May 22, 1920, and passing away in December 2013. I found a photo of her while going through old family photos—a picture of her holding a bottle of Sprite at Art and Ardis' 50th wedding anniversary celebration. It's a snapshot of a life well lived, a part of the larger story of how my family came together on Barton Road.

Photo Credit: Margi Dalgleish Roth

Chapter 11
The Hippy Mailman of Loma Linda

By Emery Rockwell

1957 Construction photograph of the Loma Linda Post Office

Photo Credit: LLU Digital Archives

In the early 1970s, my life took an unexpected turn when I landed a job in the mailroom at Loma Linda University. At the time, I had no idea that it would serve as the launchpad for a career at the United States Postal Service, a retirement job with UPS, or that the stories I gathered there would still make me smile decades later.

I was going to school and working nights in the University Hospital Cafeteria's dish room when I learned I was going to be a dad. By the time our son was born, I had been proudly promoted as the "Dish room Supervisor". More responsibility with no extra pay. Since I wouldn't be 18 for another year, I was only making 1.65 an hour, minimum wage for a minor. I had asked for a raise, to no avail. My friend, William Hulse, mom worked in the Campus mailroom, she told her boss about me and he offered me a job at the higher adult minimum wage. When my current boss learned of this she capitulated and offered me the same. But it was a no brainer for me. I'd rather be a Mailman than a dishwasher.

I'd been a rebellious teen and grew my hair long during my last few years at Loma Linda Academy, wearing a short hair wig to conform with the dress code. So, needless to say, I didn't exactly fit the traditional mold of an employee at an Adventist university. I knew that my long hair, tied back into a ponytail that nearly reached my waist, would make me stand out in the conservative world of Loma Linda, and possibly not in a good way. But to my surprise, the nickname "hippie mailman" seemed more endearing than divisive. People seemed to like me despite—or maybe because of—my unconventional appearance. Even my boss, Mr. McConnell, never gave me grief about my hair. In fact, I don't remember him ever mentioning it. He was a kind man, nearing retirement, who trusted me to get the job done. That trust made me want to excel.

The mailroom was a lively, bustling place. My day started early, sorting mail into pigeonholes for delivery across the sprawling campus. Twice a day, we loaded up the Cushman cart—a tiny, three-wheeled vehicle that served as one of our mail trucks and zipped around to departments, offices, and buildings. The morning route handled incoming mail, while the afternoon run focused on interoffice correspondence. I became a familiar sight, flying around town in that Cushman, sometimes on only two wheels around the corners, as I cruised around campus.

The nickname "hippie mailman" was coined by the students and faculty, and I kinda liked it. My hair, which I kept tied back while on duty, didn't bother anyone. In fact, people seemed to appreciate my friendly, laid-back approach to work. I found that surprising in a community known for its strict standards, but it made me feel at home in a way I hadn't expected.

Mr McConnell encouraged me to learn every job there. Eventually I spent more time inside, running the postage machines on a ton of outgoing mail and sorting the incoming. My official title in the mailroom became "Nixie Clerk," a role that required me to sort out undeliverable mail. Loma Linda University received all kinds of letters and packages, many addressed to no one in particular. Some simply said, "Loma Linda University" or "Loma Linda Medical Center." My job was to open these mystery items and figure out where they were supposed to go. Over time, I developed a knack for it and didn't open all of them, most went to Admissions, and I could figure out the rest by the return address. But every now and then, I'd come across something unique—a puzzle to solve. It was like being a detective, and I loved it.

The outgoing mail was another adventure. The university generated a significant amount mail, some of which were registered and international mail, and required special handling. These items couldn't just be dropped off at the post office's back dock; they had to be hand-delivered to the front counter. That's how I got to know the crew at the Loma Linda Post Office. For three years I was there almost daily. One day, one of the clerks asked me a life-changing question: "So, when are you going to come work with us?"

1964 photograph of the Loma Linda Post Office

Photo Credit: LLU Digital Archives

At first, I laughed it off. But they pointed to the notice hanging on the wall. The pay listed—$5.02 an hour—it was more than double what I was making in the mailroom. The idea of a steady, better-paying job was too tempting to ignore. I took the postal exam and passed. Then, with possibly a little insider manipulation and encouragement,

I was hired. That set me on a path that would define my career for the next 41 years.

Now, Loma Linda was one of only three Post Offices in the nation to deliver the mail on Sunday instead of Saturday. (The other two were Angwin California and Collegedale Tennessee.) In 1970 the city of Loma Linda was incorporated. Also, in 1971 the U.S. Post Office Department became the U.S. Postal Service, still a federal agency but one expected to be self-sufficient, not relying on taxpayers dollars. During this time there was talk of changing mail delivery to Saturday. It would save money as the Post Office was paying a 25 percent premium for anyone who had to work on Sunday. (It's still that way today)

In Loma Linda, mail had been delivered on Sunday since the 1930's. But things were changing. When I started at the post office there were only two "other" Adventists. One was the soon-to-be retired Postmaster and the last Postmaster of Loma Linda to be politically appointed. The other was the Delivery Supervisor who also had been my drill instructor in Pathfinders ten years earlier. After he retired, we were left with only one Sabbath keeping employee, a mailman who was a member of the Seventh day church of God and not an SDA. Also, the town's residents seemed to be loosening up. I mean, the ones who would go to the Campus or hospital Cafeteria for lunch after church, could now be spotted instead at the Marie Callenders in Redlands. If you catch my drift.

Anyway, I don't know what happened in Angwin or Collegedale, but in 2017, a whole thirteen years after I finally retired, I was surprised to hear on the news that the Loma

Linda Post Office was finally going to start delivering on Saturday. I'd always thought it would happen sooner. I do remember feeling sad. I figured it probably didn't matter much to anyone anymore, except to the Mail Carriers, due to the loss of their Sunday premium pay.

I still feel kinda sad. In my mind, the fact that everything shut down on Saturday, including the U.S. Post Office, made Loma Linda special and unique. End of an era, I guess.

My early days at the post office were anything but smooth. Like all new hires, I started by delivering the mail. The Delivery Supervisor had this thing about us maintaining the trucks. He reminded me personally to check the gas gage daily. So, what did I do? Of course, I ran out of gas in the middle of a route. Not once but twice in my first my first month.

The first time was on the north side of Barton Road, close to Anderson Street, in front of a bunch of apartments. I walked up to an apartment with an open door. Just as I got there, a young guy was leaving. I could hear voices from further inside, but the living room was empty. I spotted a phone. While I made the dreaded call to my boss, a few other guys came by without a glance my way. Loma Linda's version of a frat house, I guessed. And the boss was super mad and yelled at me. I deserved it.

The second time that I ran out of gas was in front of a nice condo. This time I had to knock. It's hard to describe the welcome I received. The place was full of middle-aged ladies, (three maybe), and they welcomed me enthusiastically. It made me uncomfortable. I said I couldn't stay, just needed a quick phone call. I think I drank some lemonade; it was all a blur. I knew that I was in serious trouble, now, but also when I called the boss. But when I told him the address, he broke out laughing. Seems he knew who lived there and apparently these gals were well known. At least to him. Small town for sure.

When I got back, I was thankful that I chose the right door to knock on as the boss was too anxious to hear my story than be mad. I kept him that way as long as possible. I might have embellished a bit. I don't remember him yelling at me that time, but I never ran out of gas again.

Another day, as I approached a house, a small poodle began barking at me from behind a closed screen door. I couldn't deliver the mail through the mail slot on the open door. I should have just taken the mail back to the Post office, which happened to be right across the street. But for some reason, unknown to me, then or now, I took my can of mace and sprayed him right through the screen door. That shut him up. I then opened the screen door and threw the mail inside on the floor and left. Within ten minutes I was hurrying through the backdoor of the post office and wasn't surprised to hear the phone ringing on the supervisor's desk. No one was there so I picked up the receiver, and on the other end was the poodle's furious owner. "I can't believe your mailman maced my dog!" they exclaimed. Thinking quickly, I pretended to be the supervisor. I assured them that the situation would be handled, that the mailman would be reprimanded—or possibly fired—and that we took their complaint very seriously. They seemed satisfied, and I hung up the phone, knowing I'd just dodged a bullet. I felt kinda bad about it. I still do. If this was your poodle, I'm sorry. I was young.

The mailroom and the post office taught me more than just how to sort and deliver mail. They were places where I learned about people, problem-solving, and the importance of a good sense of humor. Back at the mailroom, my reputation as the "hippie mailman" wasn't just about my hair. I think people liked me because I took my job seriously and always tried to do my best. I was friendly and laid back. After several months at the Post Office, I cut my hair (under subtle pressure from the postmaster) and started working inside at the service counter. I tried to keep that same attitude with me. But for a while I felt like I was wearing a disguise and noticed that some people treated me differently. (Better) For a few years I was the go-to guy for information on that lost classmate or mutual friend. It seemed that eventually everyone came in the post office. So, I'd have seen them or at least heard about them.

I think often about those early days and how they shaped the rest of my life. Working in the mailroom at Loma Linda University was more than just a job—it was an adventure. I'll never forget the satisfaction of seeing my name in the university directory: "Emery Rockwell, Mailroom, Nixie Clerk." That might seem small, but to me, it was proof that I was part of something bigger than myself.

When I look back on the journey from the mailroom to the post office, I see more than just a career progression. I see a collection of stories, each one filled with humor, lessons, and memories that I wouldn't trade for anything. Whether it was figuring out where a piece of lost mail belonged, zipping around campus on a Cushman cart, or misdealing with an obnoxious poodle, those moments taught me to roll with the punches and find joy in the everyday.

I've been married to my "Academy sweetheart" for 54 years now. We count 15 grandchildren, (one of whom is a mailman), and six great grandkids. Although we moved away 42 years ago, I'll always have a soft spot in my heart for my hometown and all its history. Remembering makes me smile. Thanks for listening.

Chapter 12

Peterson Tract

The story of the Peterson Tract begins on January 8, 1909, with one of the largest real estate transactions in the region at the time. The old Doran Ranch, a sprawling 55-acre citrus farm in San Bernardino, changed hands for a reported $60,000. The buyer, J.D. Langford, acquired a property rich in Valencia oranges, with a crop valued at approximately $10,000. More than just a grove, the deal secured valuable water rights from Mill Creek and the Zanja, essential for sustaining the citrus farm. The orchard itself had an interesting history, initially planted with seedlings that were later budded over to the more desirable Valencias.

By 1945, the land had exchanged hands once more. This time, Oscar Peterson, a wholesale lumber dealer from Compton, purchased 50 acres of the citrus groves from the

J.D. Langford estate. Peterson, aiming to consolidate his holdings, parted with a separate 20-acre orchard at Orange Street and Pioneer Avenue to acquire the property. His newly obtained land was primarily Valencia oranges, benefiting from a well for irrigation, a crucial asset in California's often-dry climate. The grove had a non-cultivation system in place, and heaters had been installed to guard against frost, a frequent threat to citrus growers.

Nestled along Mountain View Avenue, the property had well-established citrus groves, with some trees dating back to the 1920s. Some of the oldest trees had been producing fruit for over three decades, while others had been planted after Langford acquired the property. As a consistent producer of citrus crops, the land was not only valuable but also a lucrative investment. However, the winds of change were beginning to blow through Southern California, and agriculture was steadily giving way to urban expansion.

By 1949, the inevitable shift from agriculture to development was underway. Plans were submitted to convert the land into a 50-acre residential and industrial subdivision. The proposal included 213 lots, with eight of the largest fronting Colton Avenue, designated for business or industrial use. The rest were intended for single-family and multi-family dwellings. The project signaled a major shift, reflecting the postwar boom that was transforming California.

Peterson, however, did not build houses on Colton Avenue, which at the time was also Highway 99 and later became Redlands Boulevard. He saw those lots as prime real estate for commercial endeavors, holding onto them rather than developing residential properties there. This decision left the main thoroughfare open for future business ventures, anticipating the commercial needs of the growing community.

The Peterson Tract became the first major housing development in Loma Linda. The initial phase of the tract included about 60 homes. Oscar Peterson, with his background in wholesale lumber, had an advantage in securing materials for construction. My grandfather, an electrical contractor, was contacted by Peterson to wire the homes. At that point, he had never worked on a housing tract before, but he took on the challenge.

Construction of the homes was a complex dance of different trades, each playing a critical role in bringing the neighborhood to life. The framers were the first to arrive, transforming empty lots into skeletal structures with speed and precision. They worked in teams, hammering together the wooden frameworks that would support the walls, ceilings, and roofs. The concrete crews followed closely behind, pouring sturdy foundations that needed to set just right before the next phase of construction could begin.

The plumbers and sheet metal workers came next, installing the intricate network of pipes and ventilation systems that would provide running water, gas, and proper air circulation. My grandfather and my Uncle Don worked alongside these trades, carefully running electrical wiring through the walls before the plasterers arrived. The plasterers were experts in their own right, applying layers of wet plaster over wooden lath to create the smooth, durable walls that would stand the test of time. However, they had a bad habit of filling the electrical boxes with plaster, making it difficult for my grandfather to locate them later. Fortunately, he found a clever solution—using a large magnet that had been originally designed for WWII radar installations at the end of the war. By passing the magnet over the walls, he could detect the buried electrical boxes and clear them out, saving countless hours of frustration.

Then came the roofers, perched high above, nailing shingles in place while balancing against the elements. The finish carpenters moved in afterward, adding the fine details that gave each home its unique character—door casings, trim, and kitchen cabinetry. The painters followed, their brushes and rollers transforming the houses from bare structures into homes with personality and warmth.

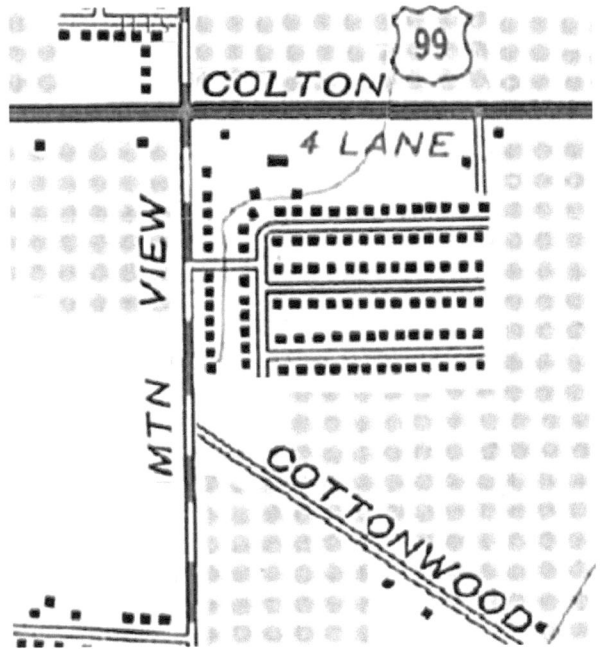

Adding to the challenge, Peterson initially proposed bartering a house or two as payment for the electrical work. While this might have been an enticing offer, my grandfather declined, a decision that turned out to be wise. He barely broke even on the project, considering the time and effort required. The cost of materials fluctuated, and unforeseen complications often led to extra expenses. Still, he took pride in his work, knowing that these homes would stand for generations.

As the project neared completion, Peterson needed workers to clean and wash all the newly installed windows. My grandfather saw an opportunity and volunteered my mother and my Aunt Betty for the job. They stuck it out for a couple of weeks, enduring long hours of cleaning in newly constructed homes. The work was tedious, requiring them to scrub away the layers of dust and debris left by the construction crews. By the end of each day, they were exhausted, but the sight of sparkling windows in freshly built homes was rewarding.

Beyond the electrical work, my grandfather also observed the overall construction process. The houses featured solid oak flooring, a feature that would become a selling point in later years. Hardwood was still widely used, and these homes were built to last. Peterson ensured that the exteriors had a uniform, attractive appearance, with simple but functional designs that catered to postwar families looking for affordable yet comfortable homes.

Beyond the pre-built homes, Peterson also began selling individual lots at the southern end of the development. Buyers had two options: they could either have Peterson build a custom home to their specifications or purchase the lot outright and hire an independent builder. The least expensive homes in the tract sold for $4,900, complete with oak hardwood floors and tile bathrooms. These homes were designed for move-in convenience—buyers simply needed to landscape the yards.

By 1951, homes in the Peterson Tract were in high demand. Advertisements in local newspapers urged prospective buyers to act quickly, as lots were selling rapidly. The community began to take shape, with families moving in and forming a tight-knit neighborhood. A local paper noted that the Dooleys had recently settled in and that if you wanted a lot, you had better move fast.

The Peterson Tract was soon bustling with life. By 1957, a typical home in the development could be purchased for $47.75 per month through a GI loan. A classified ad from the time described a typical home as featuring three bedrooms, a tile bath, oak floors, a floor furnace, and a spacious 60'x127' lot. The tract had become a sought-after residential area, a testament to its well-built homes and prime location.

As the Peterson Tract grew, it became entangled in municipal disputes. By 1972, both Redlands and Loma Linda laid claim to the jurisdiction of the area. The debate centered around "zones of influence," with Loma Linda asserting that it could serve the neighborhood better, while Redlands pointed to its existing infrastructure. The Local Agency Formation Commission (LAFC) was drawn into negotiations, attempting to mediate between the two cities.

By 1979, Peterson Tract residents resisted an effort to annex the area into Loma Linda. While the LAFC had initially supported annexation, residents successfully protested the move, fearing higher taxes and the cost of tying into Loma Linda's sewer system. As a result, the LAFC altered its recommendation, placing the tract within Loma Linda's "sphere of influence" but stopping short of requiring annexation.

Today, the Peterson Tract remains a testament to the push and pull between progress and preservation. Its history of transformation from citrus groves to a thriving residential community highlights the resilience of its residents and the challenges of municipal politics. What began as a simple real estate transaction in 1909 grew into a community that continues to evolve, balancing the legacy of its past with the realities of an ever-changing Southern California.

Chapter 13
Dick Schaefer

In Hats-Dick and Bob (or, maybe it's Bob and Dick)

There is no way I could do a book about Loma Linda without honoring the one person who knew more about it than possibly anybody ever, Richard "Dick" Schaefer. He spent his life telling stories, but not just any stories. They were the stories of a community, a faith, and an institution that many called a special place on Earth. In his calm, steady voice—sometimes at a podium, often in a book, and occasionally while fielding an impossible number of phone calls during a media storm—Schaefer became both the historian and the heartbeat of Loma Linda University Health. His life was a tapestry woven with public service, faith, scholarship, and a deep affection for the town where he was born.

It seems almost preordained that his story would start at the very institution he would later devote his career to chronicling. He and his twin brother, Bob, were born at the old Loma Linda Sanitarium in July of 1941. Though they were identical twins, they were born on different days, one just before midnight and one just after. From the very beginning, even in their sameness, there was a hint of distinction.

In later years, Dick liked to tell how his first impression of the town came at the age of five, when his parents built a house on Mountain View Avenue. Two things stood out to the young boy. The first was a strange slanted concrete berm on the edge of the hill, something he had never seen before and never forgot. The second was harder to put into words—a feeling that lingered, a sense that Loma Linda was, as he later called it, a special place on Earth. That phrase would echo across his lifetime. It became the refrain of his historical work, his public addresses, and even his casual conversations. For Schaefer, Loma Linda was not just another town; it was a stage on which divine providence, human effort, and extraordinary healing unfolded.

My own first memory of Dick takes me back to around 1959, in the old Adventist two-room schoolhouse just off Lugonia and Redlands. He and his twin brother Bob stood together, singing a song they had clearly sung many times before: "I Saw Esau Sitting on a Seesaw." It was funny, memorable, and clearly one of their signature bits—a theme song of sorts that followed them through life. The Schaefer twins were inseparable, and sometimes indistinguishable. They looked so alike that only a small scar on one cheek set them apart. I think it was Dick's scar, but to this day I'm not entirely certain. I once asked Dick if he ever used his brother's identity to his advantage. With a sly grin, he just mumbled something about doing it "occasionally, when it was convenient."

His formal education took him through La Sierra College, where he graduated in 1966 with a bachelor's degree in communication. Almost immediately, he was hired by Loma Linda University as an assistant in the University Relations office. It was a modest start, but the role suited him. He was curious, diligent, and possessed a natural talent for making complex stories clear and meaningful. By the mid-1970s, he had risen to become director of Community Relations. The title made him the public face of Loma Linda University Medical Center, the man reporters called when something important—or controversial—was happening.

And then came 1984, the year that thrust both Loma Linda and Schaefer into the global spotlight. That was the year of the famous "Baby Fae" infant heart transplant, when Dr. Leonard Bailey and his team attempted to save a dying newborn by transplanting a baboon heart into her chest. For weeks, the world's media camped on the Loma Linda campus, clamoring for updates. Schaefer was the one standing in the gap, handling as many as 1,500 calls a day from reporters. He became the calm center of the storm, fielding questions with grace and representing both the institution and its mission with dignity. Many administrators would have wilted under such pressure. Schaefer, however, treated it as simply another story that needed to be told—carefully, honestly, and with a respect for both the medical team and the desperate family whose plight had captured the world's attention.

While the wider world knew him as a polished spokesman, I got to know Dick in a different setting. Around 1969, he was building a house in Forest Falls. As a young, green teenager looking for work, I was hired to help him wire the place. It was during that project that I really came to like him. He was easy to be around, with a sense of humor that could make even an ordinary Sunday job memorable. I remember one day he hobbled up the stairs, looked at me, and said with mock seriousness, "I've got a dumb feeling in the back of my leg." I asked him how I was supposed to respond to that. He replied, equally baffled, "I don't have any idea either." On another day, we needed supplies, so we drove down to Polar Electric in Yucaipa, the company his dad co-owned. He had a key to the place, so we let ourselves in. Two things stick in my mind from that drive: First, as we approached the Mill Creek Road turnoff to Forest Falls, Dick simply sailed through the stop sign without slowing down. I stared at him in shock, and he just shrugged. "Well, there was nobody coming either way. No reason for me to lose 30 seconds and grind down my brakes when it's not necessary." I had to admit, it made a certain kind of sense. The second memory was a spirited debate we had about Elvis Presley. I was into '60s music; he was a dyed-in-the-wool Elvis fan. Neither of us convinced the other, but Dick's explanation summed it up: "He's from my generation." That was that. When we were finishing the wiring on his house, he called me one evening in a panic. "Every time I turn on the porch light," he said, "the garbage disposal starts running." I was completely flummoxed, but I immediately blamed him, pointing out that he had wired half the house too. We eventually figured it out—though not without a lot of laughter at our own expense.

His twin Bob, who I came to know well, often contrasted his own working life with his brother's career path. I worked for Brother Bob at Apollo Mobile Home Supply, and I remember one blistering summer afternoon on a roof, struggling through the misery of putting on a new roof in the heat. Bob wiped the sweat from his brow, frustration in his voice, and said, "How come I couldn't get the breaks my brother got? Can you believe what he fell into? He's supposed to just speak on behalf of Loma Linda University and do their PR and keep records. How much more of a cushy job could you have gotten?" It was said half in jest, half in real exasperation, but it perfectly captured the contrast between the dusty, difficult trades and the polished professional life Dick had carved out.

Schaefer's career in public relations gave him the tools of communication. But it was his growing passion for history that defined his later years. The turning point came when he inherited the job of giving new-employee orientations. To do that well, he needed to know the story of Loma Linda. So he dug into the archives, pored over board minutes, and pieced together the remarkable tale of a fledgling institution that had survived against improbable odds. What started as preparation for orientation sessions soon became his calling. In 1977, Schaefer published the first edition of "Legacy: Daring to Care – The Heritage of Loma Linda University Medical Center." It was part history lesson, part love letter, and part devotional reflection on the faith that had guided the institution. The book proved so popular that it went through six editions, with over 300,000 copies in circulation worldwide. He went on to write much more: "On Becoming Shryock," "Glory of the Vision" (a five-volume history), "Creation: Behold, It Was Very Good," and "Of the Highest Order," a centennial book for the School of Medicine. Each carried his fingerprints: meticulous research, clear prose, and a deep sense that the story of Loma Linda was part of God's larger story.

Though his books were his most enduring contributions, Schaefer never limited himself to academic writing. He was a familiar figure in the broader community—serving on the boards of Arrowhead United Way and United Way of the East Valley, as a commissioner for the Forest Falls Fire Protection District, and as president of the Loma Linda Chamber of Commerce. He also launched a Facebook page called "You May Be From Loma Linda If." At some point, without warning, I began getting emails saying I was the administrator. It turned out that when he learned of his illness, Dick quietly appointed me to take over the page. I've tried to honor him by keeping it alive, though I changed the name to "I Remember Loma Linda"—a little less formal, a little less bulky, but always true to his spirit.

The bond between the brothers never lessened, even as their paths diverged. In an article Dick wrote after Bob's death in 2016, he reflected on their twinhood with warmth and humor. He recalled how Bob delighted in dressing alike when they traveled, buying matching hats and shirts at EPCOT so they could confuse strangers and pose for pictures with tourists. He wrote of their encounter with the Stater Bros.—the twin founders of the grocery chain—when the Schaefer brothers were cleaning windows at a store construction site. He marveled at how they both lost their hearing, their hair, and even developed skin cancer on their chins at the same time. He admitted that their mother only confused them twice in a lifetime, and with a touch of wonder, described how Bob once unlocked his iPhone with his fingerprint. His reflections revealed as much about Dick as they did about Bob: his affection, his wit, his storyteller's instinct for detail, and his gratitude for the bond they shared. Bob was his best friend, and when Dick died a year later, it was as if part of him had gone on ahead.

Schaefer's professional life was impressive, but he never lost his personal touch. He could laugh at himself, whether wearing a button that read "I'm not Bob!" to clear up twin confusion or ribbing me over wiring mistakes. He was a good guy—likable, approachable, quick to share a story or listen to yours. He had passions beyond writing: nature photography, wood turning, camping, and amateur radio. He held an Extra Class license with the call sign WM6X and even volunteered as an FCC examiner. He was as comfortable in a forest clearing with a ham radio as he was behind a lectern.

In later years, Schaefer battled leukemia. Even as his health declined, he continued writing, speaking, and sharing the story of Loma Linda. When he passed away on October 23, 2021, at the age of 80, tributes poured in. Colleagues remembered his steady leadership during times of crisis. Students and readers praised his books for giving them context and meaning. Community leaders honored his decades of service. And friends, like me, simply mourned a man whose presence had been a constant in our lives. I often wish he were still around, not only to fact-check me when I stumble on the details of Loma Linda's history but also to provide the right words when I can't find them. He had that gift.

Schaefer's life could be summed up in the phrase he repeated so often: a special place on Earth. For him, those words applied to Loma Linda. But for many who knew him, the phrase could just as easily describe Dick himself. He made the world feel more special—by telling its stories, preserving its history, and living his life with purpose. And for those of us fortunate enough to know him personally, the memories—from wiring a house in Forest Falls to debating Elvis to sharing the stewardship of a community's history—are reminders that sometimes the historian becomes part of the history he tells. For me, there will never be another quite like him, and this book is as much his as it is mine.

Chapter 14

Nelson Plumbing

By: Genie Nelson Sample

Photo Credit: Genie Nelson Sample

My father, Stan Nelson, was born on April 9, 1926, in Lucknow, India. His childhood was spent in India, where his parents were missionaries. My grandfather was a minister, and he and my grandmother started their married life there, raising their five sons and one daughter before eventually returning to the States. My dad attended Vincent Hill School, a boarding school in India, where he was known as a prankster. One of his favorite stories was about how he rigged the dormitory lights so that he could turn them on remotely after lights out, much to the confusion of the staff. They would turn the lights off, and he would turn them right back on, leaving them baffled until they finally figured out that it was him.

Despite coming from a family of medical professionals, my dad realized early on that medicine was not for him. When he returned to the United States at 18, he initially enrolled in pre-med at La Sierra College but soon discovered that his true passion was working with his hands. He had a knack for mechanics and problem-solving, leading him to a job in the maintenance department at Loma Linda. He worked on a wide variety of tasks, becoming a jack-of-all-trades before naturally transitioning into plumbing, eventually founding Nelson Plumbing.

Nelson Plumbing started as a one-man operation, but it grew into a well-known business with a fleet of trucks and multiple employees. He became known as the Loma Linda Plumber, and his business served both residential and commercial clients. My mother played a crucial role in the business, handling billing and collections. If we needed something growing up, she would go out and collect overdue payments to ensure we had what we needed. She would personally visit customers, making sure that bills were paid so that our family could afford necessities like clothes and shoes.

My father was a man of many interests. He had a dream of becoming a commercial airline pilot and even learned to fly a small plane. He owned a Bellanca, which he flew regularly. One of my fondest memories was when he flew our family across the country to attend a wedding in Colorado. However, his piloting career ended abruptly when he experienced engine failure shortly after takeoff in Rialto, forcing him to land in a field. I remember the aftermath well. He called Mike Kunert to bring his crane truck over, load the plane onto my dad's trailer and transport it back home. The plane sat in the workshop for a long time before eventually being given to his nephew Stanley Wheeler.

The business itself went through several locations. Initially, Nelson Plumbing operated out of a building on Highway 99, which had previously been a car dealership owned by Mick Farrar. The building, with its large glass windows, provided ample space for showcasing plumbing supplies and tools. It was a well-known fixture in the community, and many people have fond memories of visiting it. My father later moved the business to Brookside Avenue before finally constructing the Butler Building, where he continued his work.

Over the years, my father explored various business ventures, including Butler Buildings and even pool installations. He was always looking for new opportunities and wasn't afraid to try different things. One of the most notable projects I remember was when he experimented with radiant heating by embedding pipes in a concrete slab at the Butler Building. He installed a massive pool heater to warm the slab, but the result was that the floor became so hot that people had to take their shoes off! Once the slab got hot, it stayed hot for a long time, making it both effective and a bit of a challenge.

My father also had a strong stance against unions. He fought numerous legal battles to keep Nelson Plumbing independent, often obtaining injunctions to prevent union interference. He was known for his clever strategies, such as scheduling early morning concrete pours so that by the time union picketers arrived, the work was already completed. He went to court many times over these issues, always standing firm in his belief that he could run his business without union involvement.

Despite his business acumen and tough stance on labor issues, my father was a deeply compassionate man. He was known for hiring people who were struggling and giving them opportunities to work. At one point, he even bought a building that housed a group of young hippies and offered them a place to stay on the condition that they attend weekly Bible studies with him. Though the results were mixed—one of them ultimately gave up, and another tragically took his own life—it was a testament to his commitment to helping others.

Nelson Plumbing remained a staple in the community for many years, and my father's impact is still remembered. Even after he moved the business, the old building on Highway 99 remained a landmark. There was even an incident where a car crashed into the front of the building, destroying the facade. I still remember the chaos that followed, as we received a call in the middle of the night and later surveyed the extensive damage in the morning. The crash left everything scattered, and it took quite a while to repair the damage.

Photo Credit: Genie Nelson Sample

He had a number of employees over the years, some of whom left a lasting impression. There was also one employee who unfortunately stole copper pipes from the business to make money. My father was incredibly patient, but had to deal with a variety of workplace challenges.

Another notable aspect of his work was that he played a role in the local plumbing and contracting community. He worked alongside other well-known plumbers like George Randolph, Larry Cole, and Sam Donnelly. Many of these men had once worked for him before going off on their own. The area around his business became something of a hub for contractors. Cabinet makers like Wayne Westfall and EV builder Maurice Woods, and even electricians like Ed Buschbacher, Steve Dacre, and Mike Kunert, all had shops nearby. It was a tightly knit business community where everyone knew each other.

Through all the ups and downs, my father remained dedicated to his work and his family. He was an entrepreneur, a mentor, and a man of integrity. Though he has since passed, his legacy lives on in the countless homes and buildings he worked on, and in the stories of those who knew him. Nelson Plumbing wasn't just a business; it was a testament to my father's skill, determination, and unwavering work ethic. His impact reached beyond just the services he provided—he was a pillar of the community, a man whose influence is still felt today.

Chapter 15

The Emmersons and the Bartletts

By Vicki and Kandy Bartlett

Photo Credit: Kandy Bartlett

In 1928, Richard Fillmore Emmerson, known as R.F. to his friends and family, decided to open a market in Loma Linda. This was no ordinary corner store—it was a full-service establishment that seemed to have something for everyone. The Emmerson Market sold dry goods, groceries, and even vegetarian foods from Battle Creek, a staple in the local diet. But it wasn't just a market; it also had a gas station that sold gasoline, diesel, and marine gas oil, along with a soda fountain and lunch counter that quickly became the heart of the operation.

The market sat in what is now the general area of Loma Linda University's School of Dentistry, near where the power plant would later be built. Photos from the time show a classic small-town commercial hub, with apartments upstairs, a barber shop, and even a shoe repair shop. And if you needed a book or a Bible, you could stop by the Book and Bible House store next to the power plant. A gas station rounded out the little cluster of businesses, making the area a one-stop shop for just about anything a local might need.

When R.F.'s son, Glenn Emmerson, married Inez in 1929, he was given the responsibility of running the soda fountain and lunch counter. It seemed like a perfect setup for a young couple, providing a steady business and a place to live in the cottages on the property.

But Glenn, never one to leave well enough alone, decided to experiment with the store's offerings. One of his more infamous attempts at innovation involved using one of the ice cream vats to try his hand at brewing beer. This was during Prohibition, of course, which made the whole operation even more questionable.

Glenn's experiment didn't go well. In fact, it went so badly that it ended in an explosion. Whether the mixture was too potent or the vat simply wasn't designed for beer fermentation, the results were disastrous. The explosion sent ingredients flying and made such a racket that Glenn had to lock the doors to keep his mother, Lottie, from barging in to investigate. While she was busy trying to determine the source of the commotion, Glenn was desperately trying to clean up the mess before anyone found out.

Photo Credit: Kandy Bartlett

No word on whether he ever tried his hand at brewing again, but it's safe to say that his soda fountain experiment would go down in Emmerson family history as an absolute failure.

By 1933, Glenn had grown tired of the soda shop and decided to switch careers—dramatically. He took a job at Shaw's Mortuary in San Bernardino, where he started as an ambulance driver and gradually learned the funeral business. Wanting to take his training further, he went to embalming school in Los Angeles.

His father, R.F., saw the opportunity for a family business, and together they invested $45,000 to build what would become Emmerson Mortuary in Redlands in 1935. It was a complete operation, including a funeral home and an ambulance service. Glenn and Inez moved into the apartment above the mortuary, and their daughter, Vicki, was born in 1933.

Growing up in a mortuary had its quirks. As a child, Vicki was given small tasks like dusting furniture in the lobby. She quickly discovered that the chairs and pews in the funeral home had a hidden benefit—people's loose change would often slip out of their pockets and fall between the cushions. Vicki became quite the entrepreneur, gathering up the coins and spending them at local stores in Redlands.

When it came time to get her driver's license, Vicki had an unconventional vehicle for her driving test—a seven-passenger funeral limousine. The sight of a teenager pulling up for her test in a massive limo must have been quite a moment for the examiner, but she passed, proving she could handle just about any vehicle.

Meanwhile, Glenn's brother, Harland Emmerson, was carving out his own path in life. Though he was involved in the family business, his heart was always set on something else—owning a ranch. Harland co-owned the mortuary properties with his father and brother, but his passion lay outside the funeral industry. Eventually, he pursued his dream, buying a sheep ranch that would become a whole new chapter of adventure for him and his family.

As the business grew, so did the family's ambitions. In 1955, the Emmersons purchased land next to Montecito Memorial Park in Loma Linda and built a brand-new facility, naming it Emmerson Valley Mortuary. It was a strategic move—being right next to a cemetery certainly had its advantages for a funeral home.

At the same time, Glenn and his family remained deeply involved in the local community. Long before he became a funeral director, Glenn had managed a Loma Linda baseball team in 1929, leading them to win the Redlands City Championship. He was also a member of just about every organization in the area, from the Elks Club to the Kiwanis to the Redlands Rotary. He even served on the Redlands City Council and as a San Bernardino County Sheriff's Reserve.

By the early 1960s, Glenn had expanded the business further, this time bringing his son-in-law, Richard "Dick" Bartlett, into the fold. The Bartlett family had a long entrepreneurial history of their own, having owned businesses in Big Bear, including a general store and Cedar Lake, which they later sold to a movie studio.

To reflect the partnership, the family rebranded the business as Emmerson Bartlett Mortuaries. Now operating in four locations—Redlands, Yucaipa, Loma Linda, and Calimesa—they had firmly established themselves in the region.

But the story doesn't end there. Years later, Glenn's grandson, Rick, followed in the family tradition by attending Loma Linda University's School of Dentistry. One day, he met a fellow student, and their families eventually gathered for a meal. That's when a surprising connection was discovered—Rick's father, Dick, and his future wife's father, Howard Welklin, had already met many times before, riding together in a funeral limousine to graveside services.

Rick and his future wife hit it off, but there was one small problem—Rick only owned a motorcycle. Not exactly the best mode of transportation for a first date. So, in true Emmerson-Bartlett fashion, he borrowed the family mortuary sedan. And that's how a young couple's first date happened in a funeral home vehicle—because nothing says romance like a borrowed hearse-adjacent car.

By 1981, after decades of serving Loma Linda and surrounding communities, the Emmerson and Bartlett families decided to sell the funeral businesses to a Texas-based company that was acquiring Montecito Memorial Park. Though they initially only wanted to purchase the Loma Linda location, they ended up buying all four mortuaries. However, the Emmersons and Bartletts retained ownership of the Redlands and Yucaipa properties, continuing their legacy as landlords.

After retiring, Dick and Vicki Bartlett embraced their love of travel, taking their RV across the country multiple times. Even into their eighties, they were still skiing with friends in Angel Fire, New Mexico, proving that retirement didn't mean slowing down.

Meanwhile, Glenn and his father's contributions to Loma Linda lived on. From their early days running the market near the power plant to their decades of funeral service, their presence had shaped the town in ways big and small. Glenn's ill-fated beer experiment in the ice cream vat remains a legendary tale of good intentions gone spectacularly wrong, a reminder that even in a family of serious businesspeople, a little bit of mischief and experimentation was never too far away.

Chapter 16

Smitty the Barber

By Scott Smith

Photo Credit: Scott Smith

My dad, Duane Smith—better known around town as *Smitty the Barber*—wasn't born with scissors in his hands. But you wouldn't know it from the way he made that barber chair spin like a carnival ride and turned every haircut into a full-blown conversation. His journey into barbering wasn't a straight line—it was more like a wild cloverleaf off the 10 Freeway, full of bumps, blessings, and more than a few back-snapping detours.

Dad was born in 1932 in Utah, the youngest of five boys. When he was about seven, his father left the family for another woman—ironically, her name was Edna too, just like my grandma. After the split, Grandma packed up all five boys and moved them to a tiny two-bedroom house on North Evans Street in Loma Linda. She never drove a car, but walked all the way up the hill every day to work as a nurse at the old hospital. She was a saint. That house may have been small, but the dreams inside were anything but.

Dad struggled in school. He didn't read well, and an early teacher angered my grandmother by telling her he wasn't very smart and wouldn't amount to much in life. Although he never went to college and only earned a high school equivalency, he proved to be incredibly intelligent in practical matters. He became a jack of all trades—learning plumbing, landscaping, painting, mechanics, and even animal husbandry. He liked work—and made sure his kids did way more of it than we thought was appropriate.

Later, Dad worked for a plumber in Maryland, where he slipped on some icy stairs while carrying a bathtub. He didn't know it at the time, but he had broken his back. He kept working anyway. A chiropractor made things worse, and eventually the pain drove him back to Loma Linda. With the help of Dr. Richard Walden, he was properly diagnosed and underwent spinal fusion surgery. This was back when they wrapped you in a full-body cast and stuck you in bed for half a year. He had to learn to walk all over again.

Hard labor was out, and sitting too long was torture. Someone suggested barber school. It seemed like a strange fit at first, but it turned out to be the perfect career for him. He studied in Los Angeles first, when we lived on San Mateo Street. We were dirt poor. We also lost a baby brother to SIDS during that time.

Eventually, Dad transferred to the newly opened barber school in San Bernardino. He passed the California Barber Board exam with the second-highest score ever recorded at the time. He got a job with Frank Boadway at his uptown barbershop and worked there for five or six years. Frank treated him well, but other shop politics made things uncomfortable. So when the opportunity came to open a new shop in Redlands with brand-new equipment, Dad jumped at it. He partnered with Larry Vagelin, who later decided to work only at the Redlands shop. That left Dad running the San Juan Barbershop on his own—and he thrived.

Over the years, he brought in other barbers—Halstead, Roundtree, George with the big beard, and Frank Mott. Eventually, he bought the building from a couple who owned a dry cleaner in Colton. Next door, the Westerbergs ran the company's cleaner outlet store. I worked for them one summer, and my sister Shirley took over their business when Dad bought the building.

But our family story took a real turn during Dad's recovery from surgery. Mom applied to be on the show *Queen for a Day*. She told her story—not with tears, but matter-of-fact, like she always did—and the applause meter went wild. She won. That brought us a windfall of custom prizes: a barber chair, professional equipment, jewelry, luggage, a TV, and some cash. Dad even traded that big console TV to Dr. Jesse to help pay off part of the surgery bill.

Photo Credit: Scott Smith

After that, we scraped together enough money to buy a lot up on Lawton. With help from Dr. Walden and builder Joe Mays, we built a home up there among the jackrabbits and rattlesnakes. People used to call it Snob Hill, but it felt like the top of the world to us.

Dad barbered in Loma Linda until 1977, when I graduated from dental school and he retired to a 40-acre farm in the Walla Walla Valley of Washington. But he couldn't quite hang up the clippers. He kept barbering in College Place for another 15 years while working the farm with his brother.

Later, he retired to San Pasqual near Escondido, where he grew everything from avocados and citrus to macadamia nuts. Just a year and a half after he sold that place, the massive fire of 2007 swept through and leveled the property.

He would've stayed to defend it too, knowing him—but fortunately, he was long gone by then.

After Escondido, he moved to Sequim, Washington, then to Arizona. After Mom passed away six years ago, we brought him up here and built him a small apartment next to my shop. He just turned 93 last week—and yep, he's still chugging along.

One of his favorite barbershop stories was about a guy who came in with a comb-over that stretched all the way across his shiny dome. Frank Mott was cutting his hair and said, "Joe, you're not fooling anybody with that comb-over. Let me cut it off." The guy lit up red from neck to forehead, stormed out of the chair, and barked, "Sonny, I'll have hair on my head even if I have to train it from my armpits!"

Dad had his share of tussles with City Hall too. In the mid-'70s, there was a zoning battle over his barbershop. The city planner and some councilmembers wanted to de-zone his property from commercial use. He fought back—passionately—and with help from friends like Clifford Dinning and Mayor Dickinson, he narrowly won the vote. That decision allowed him to sell the building and business when he moved to Washington.

I worked one summer next door at the dry cleaner and could hear everything through the common wall. He had this masterful way of recycling stories—just enough variety to keep them fresh until the same customers came back. His repertoire was like a sitcom: classic punchlines, predictable timing, and always a great payoff.

And yes, there was a chart on the wall of flat tops and butch haircuts. He sold Butch Wax too. I've got pictures of myself in those stiff, spiky cuts. My favorite part was when he'd snap the comb against the back of my head and say, "You're outta here, bud—it's good enough for who it's for."

First time I had him in my dental chair, I returned the favor. Sat him up, tapped him on the head, and said, "You're outta here, Pop. It's good enough for who it's for." He cracked up.

Dad had a lot of good friends in Loma Linda—your grandfather, Amos Giberson, included. He thought the world of him. People like Dr. Robert Rosenquist and Dr. Richard Walden—they weren't just clients, they were part of the barbershop family. His shop was kind of like *Cheers,* but with clippers instead of cocktails. A regular cast of characters, everybody knew everybody, and you never left without a story.

Dad's brothers were quite a group, too. The oldest, Elden, was a missionary in Thailand; Darrell was a Bible teacher and pastor; Merlin was an orthopedic surgeon with 13 kids—yep, married a Mormon woman; and Milton was a teacher in several towns before retiring in Kansas. All of them lived into their 90s, except for Darrell. Dad's gunning for the record.

Photo Credit: Scott Smith

I was born in the old hospital. I remember walking home through orange groves where the new hospital now stands, throwing rotten oranges and firecrackers like we were in some kind of citrus-based war zone. I broke my arm in first grade and went under general anesthesia with ether—still remember waking up spinning and nauseous, with that dreamlike smell.

And oh, the dogs. I ended up in the ER twice from Great Dane bites—once at Roxanne Warner's house when I accidentally got too close to some puppies, and the other time up on Anderson Street with a German dentist's dog. After that, I started carrying a big pipe and some rocks anytime I visited. I was ready.

You know what's funny? I remember all the good stuff. The bad stuff? It kind of fades away. Maybe that's the best thing about growing up in a place like Loma Linda. We had barbers, neighbors, stories, and dogs with too many teeth—but through it all, there was always laughter. Always connection.

Smitty the Barber may have started out with a broken back and a borrowed dream, but he carved out a life that touched just about everyone in town. And now, even at 93, his stories are still razor sharp.

Photo Credit: Scott Smith

Chapter 17

The Story of Pigeon Pass Road

On April 10, 1916, *The Colton Courier* celebrated a milestone for San Bernardino County:

"The Pigeon Pass Road to Riverside, which is now being paved as far as the Riverside County line under the highway bond issue of the county, will be open for traffic in ten days or two weeks, unless rain stops the work that is being pushed as rapidly as possible."

This stretch of road, once an unremarkable rural route, had become indispensable for the region. During heavy rains, Pigeon Pass Road was the only viable exit out of Redlands, while other roads and railways succumbed to flooding. Supplies and essential goods traveled over its uneven terrain to reach stranded communities.

Photo Credit: Caltrans

The bond-funded improvements in 1916 promised to transform the pass into an "all-paved highway from Redlands to Riverside." Its new macadam surface would provide a reliable, year-round connection between the two cities. These enhancements marked an important step forward for regional infrastructure, reflecting a growing need for better roads as automobiles became increasingly common.

Pigeon Pass Road was more than a means of travel; it was a vital lifeline during times of crisis. The rainy season of 1916 had demonstrated its importance as the only viable route for transporting supplies when other means failed. Its improvement was not just a matter of convenience but one of necessity.

By 1921, Pigeon Pass Road had cemented its reputation as a critical transportation link. However, maintaining its macadam surface was no small feat. Wear and tear from vehicles, coupled with the natural settling of the roadbed, left the surface rough and uneven. To tackle this problem, San Bernardino County introduced a groundbreaking solution: a specialized highway maintenance machine.

Photo Credit: Caltrans

The machine, a combination of a truck, disc, and grader, was designed to smooth out the bumps that formed in the oil-treated macadam surface. Operated by only two men, it was cost-effective and efficient. Its first deployment was on Pigeon Pass Road, which was considered the roughest stretch of macadam in the county. The disc shaved off irregularities, while the grader re-leveled the roadbed, returning the road to better-than-new condition.

This early investment in maintenance technology demonstrated the county's commitment to keeping Pigeon Pass Road in excellent shape, ensuring it could continue to serve as a vital artery for the region.

This innovation didn't just benefit Pigeon Pass Road; it paved the way for improved maintenance across the county. Roads that had once been considered difficult to maintain could now be kept in top condition, setting a precedent for future infrastructure projects.

Fifteen years after its initial paving, Pigeon Pass Road was due for another significant upgrade. In December 1931, San Bernardino County initiated a comprehensive project to widen and realign the road. The improvements would transform the pass into a 30-foot-wide highway, matching the newly modernized section east of Loma Linda, which had recently been hailed as one of the finest roads in the county.

The project aimed to eliminate many of the sharp curves that had long made the road dangerous and challenging to navigate. A smoother alignment and a better surface would make the pass safer and more efficient for the increasing number of drivers.

At an estimated cost of $25,000—a substantial sum at the time—the project included significant regrading and paving work. Riverside County also committed to improving its portion of the road, straightening curves past the Grand Terrace School and extending upgrades to La Cadena Drive. These collaborative efforts marked a new era for Pigeon Pass Road, reflecting the growing importance of regional connectivity.

The project didn't just benefit commuters. Local businesses and farmers also reaped the rewards of a better road. Easier transportation meant goods could be moved more efficiently, boosting the local economy and strengthening ties between communities.

Despite these advancements, by the late 1940s, Pigeon Pass Road was struggling to keep up with modern demands. The road had become a victim of its own success. Carrying thousands of vehicles daily, it faced significant wear and tear, while its outdated design no longer met contemporary safety standards.

The 8.3-mile stretch was riddled with hazards. Sharp curves, including the infamous reverse curve at Pigeon Curve and a dangerous right-angle turn in Loma Linda's business center, made navigation treacherous. The road's narrow lanes—some only 20 feet wide—added to the difficulty, especially for larger vehicles. Poor drainage exacerbated the problem, leading to pavement deterioration and further safety concerns. Pigeon Pass Road was also a school bus route and a feeder road for local farmers. It wasn't just about connecting cities; it was about connecting people to their daily lives. These roles made its improvement even more urgent.

The goal was ambitious: to create a high-standard two-lane highway that would meet the needs of a growing region. The plan called for widening the road to 30 feet, eliminating sharp curves, and adding eight-foot paved shoulders to accommodate parking. Engineers also sought to improve drainage, ensuring the road would remain durable and reliable for years to come.

One of the most significant challenges was the Gage Canal, which crossed Pigeon Pass Road at an angle near Waterman Avenue. The canal's thin cement mortar lining allowed seepage, which weakened the soil beneath the roadbed. This instability posed a serious threat to the road's longevity and required innovative engineering solutions.

Pigeon Pass Road at Waterman Ave. and the Gage Canal in Loma Linda Looking East

Photo Credit: Caltrans

Construction officially began on January 7, 1949, under the direction of Basich Bros. Construction Company from San Gabriel. Despite the project's complexity, the team completed the work ahead of schedule on September 2, 1949—an impressive feat that reflected both careful planning and efficient execution.

A key factor in the project's success was the use of advanced equipment, including continuous mixing plants that allowed workers to lay an average of 1,360 tons of asphalt daily. Dangerous curves were replaced with long-radius bends, many with a radius of 900 feet, providing smoother transitions and improved visibility for drivers. In Loma Linda, the road was rerouted through undeveloped land to avoid its hazardous right-angle turn, further enhancing safety.

The workers, too, played a vital role in the road's success. From the laborers who regraded the slopes to the engineers who solved complex drainage problems, every individual contributed to a project that would serve the community for decades to come.

As with any large-scale project, the modernization of Pigeon Pass Road faced its share of unexpected challenges. Along a 1.3-mile stretch west of Waterman Avenue, the road paralleled the Gage Canal at a lower elevation. This proximity caused unexpected soil instability, requiring additional drainage solutions and imported materials to ensure the road could handle heavy traffic without future problems.

*Pigeon Pass Road at Benton Ave. in Loma Linda
Looking East*

*Pigeon Pass Road at Nevada St. in Redlands
Looking East*

Photo Credits: Caltrans

The story of Pigeon Pass Road is more than a tale of infrastructure; it's a reflection of the Inland Empire's growth and evolution. What began as a simple rural route became a lifeline during floods, a testing ground for early road maintenance innovations, and ultimately, a modern highway that connected people and places.

The road's transformation was made possible by the vision and collaboration of local, state, and federal agencies, as well as the ingenuity of the engineers and workers who brought the project to life. Each improvement—from the introduction of the highway maintenance machine in 1921 to the comprehensive upgrades of the 1930s and 1940s—represented a step forward for the region.

Today, Barton Road continues to serve as a vital artery for the Inland Empire, bridging the past and present while paving the way for the future. It stands as a testament to the power of innovation, community investment, and the enduring importance of infrastructure in shaping our lives

With the completion of its modernization, Pigeon Pass Road was officially renamed Barton Road by the San Bernardino County Board of Supervisors. This name change honored Dr. Ben Barton, a pioneer settler, physician, agriculturist, and educator who played a vital role in the region's history. Dr. Barton's home, located on Nevada Street in San Bernardino just north of Barton Road, still stands as a testament to his contributions.

The renaming marked not just the end of a project but the beginning of a new chapter for the road and the communities it served. From its early days as a rough macadam path to its transformation into a modern two-lane highway, Pigeon Pass Road had become a symbol of progress and resilience.

The renaming also reflected the growing sense of pride in the region's history. By naming the road after a local pioneer, the county acknowledged its roots while looking toward the future.

Pigeon Pass/Barton Road near San Juan. in Loma Linda Looking West

Photo Credit: Caltrans

The story of Pigeon Pass Road is more than a tale of infrastructure; it's a reflection of the Inland Empire's growth and evolution. What began as a simple rural route became a lifeline during floods, a testing ground for early road maintenance innovations, and ultimately, a modern highway that connected people and places.

The road's transformation was made possible by the vision and collaboration of local, state, and federal agencies, as well as the ingenuity of the engineers and workers who brought the project to life. Each improvement—from the introduction of the highway maintenance machine in 1921 to the comprehensive upgrades of the 1930s and 1940s—represented a step forward for the region.

Today, Barton Road continues to serve as a vital artery for the Inland Empire, bridging the past and present while paving the way for the future. It stands as a testament to the power of innovation, community investment, and the enduring importance of infrastructure in shaping our lives.

Chapter 18

Ben Ruckle

In 1976, I landed the biggest job my company had ever had-wiring thirty-six 4-plexes in Loma Linda for a company called Rincon Development. The 4-plex in the picture is one of those.

The managing partner was an old friend of my grandfather's, and an all-around great guy named Ben Ruckle. At the time, I was learning to fly, and Ben had a Mooney airplane, which he often took on flights to Santa Barbara, where he was building a new house. The Mooney was a sweet plane—fast, with retractable gear and a variable speed prop. My only issue with Mooneys was that they looked like someone had installed the tail backward, and they shared the same name as a powerful cult at the time. During those flights, Ben and I became pretty good friends.

One day on the job, I was talking to Ben, and he asked me to step into his office. He advised me to buy one of those 4-plexes. They were selling for $119,000, but he offered me one for $100,000 with 10% down. He said they would "easily" rent for $250 a month, which was at the very high end of rentals in Loma Linda at the time. I did the math.

First, I'd need to scrape up the $10,000 for the down payment. Also, the interest rate for apartment buildings back then was 9%, which meant payments would be $750 a month—a huge amount. My payment on my Mentone house was just $99, and I'd paid only $15,000 for it two years earlier, mainly because it had a year-round stream called The Zanja running through the backyard.

After doing the math, I figured that if I got $250 a month for each apartment (which I doubted), one vacancy would mean losing my shirt because I'd still have to pay water, trash, sewer, insurance, and taxes. It looked like a bottomless money pit. I thanked Ben for the offer but declined.

Flash forward about 50 years.

Things got worse in the late '70s, and a couple of the units went into foreclosure because nobody could afford the $250 a month rent. But in the early '80s, things turned around in a big way and never stopped. If I had bought one of those units back then and kept it, today they'd be worth over a million dollars each, with rental income exceeding $100,000 per year (the original cost of the unit).

Do I regret my decision not to buy one? No. I think I still made the right decision at the time.

It does remind me of something another mentor of mine in the '70s, named Lonnie Kerby, once told me: "Never underestimate the power of real estate."

Photo Credit: Jon Ruckle

Chapter 19

KDUO

> **Adventist College Gets Radio Station**
> The Federal Communications Commission has granted permission to the Alumni Association of the College of Medical Evangelists, a Seventh-day Adventist institution, to operate an FM radio station in Riverside, California. The new station, KDUO, will specialize in programs of classical music and cultural entertainment.

On May 1, 1959, there was this little snippet in "The Signs of the Times" (A Seventh Day Adventist publication) about the College of Medical Evangelists (Now Loma Linda University) were granted a license by the FCC for an FM radio station with the assigned frequency of of 97.5 MHz. It was one of the first FM stations in the Inland Empire. The biggest obstacle they had was in 1959, almost nobody owned FM radios. They requested and received the call letters KDUO (Which stood for "Do unto others") Instead of putting the station in Loma Linda they put it at La Sierra College in La Sierra.

Things could have gone better.

A couple of years later a pair of LA businessmen named Howard Tullis and John Hearn closed a deal to buy radio station KFXM, whose studios were in the California Hotel in San Bernardino.

Apparently about that time the CME Alumni were having second thoughts about the radio business and were looking for an out. Tullis and Hearn entered the picture and "took it off their hands". They moved it to a small studio in downtown Riverside. One of the on-air people he hired was a kid with "a good voice" to play records. They called it Beautiful Music KDUO- 97.5. The center isle of your FM Dial. Tullis and Hearn were also involved in a real estate adventure near the new freeway interchange in San Bernardino. It was a new Motel which became the Holiday Inn. They thought that right next to the pool was the perfect place new studios for both stations. A few years later KFXM rocketed to #1. KDUO languished, however, playing "elevator music".

In the early 70's FM was taking over radio for music, but not wanting to give up the elevator music, the widow of one of the founders continued with the same formats as both stations rode off into the sunset.

Forward to today.

97.5 is no longer KDUO. It is KLYY. AKA **José 97.5** FM. It is by far the most listened to station In the Riverside San Bernardino Market. It is rumored to be worth well over 100 million dollars.

The kid "with the good voice" who was in high school when he worked at KDUO-went on to become the #1 DJ at KFXM. His name was, and is Don McCoy.

Chapter 20

The School of Tropical and Preventive Medicine

Photo Credit: brucehalstead.blogspot.com

The idea of a school of tropical medicine may sound exotic, but in the 1940s it grew out of something very practical. The Seventh-day Adventist church had missionaries scattered across the globe, and many of them were returning home with stories of unfamiliar diseases that crippled their work. Malaria, parasites, strange fevers — illnesses that weren't covered in the standard medical curriculum. By the middle of the decade, two young doctors, Bruce

Halstead and Harold Mozar, convinced the board at the College of Medical Evangelists that a new kind of school was needed, one that would prepare doctors not just for American clinics but for the tropics. Their proposal was approved in 1946, and on April 1, 1948, the School of Tropical and Preventive Medicine opened its doors.

In those early days, the school didn't have much in the way of prestige or money. What it did have was imagination. And at the heart of that imagination was Dr. Bruce Halstead. Halstead wasn't your typical white-coated professor. He wore bright Hawaiian shirts that made him stand out in any room. He loved the ocean and believed nature's most dangerous poisons could also be its greatest cures. His passion for discovery was infectious, and he gave the School its energy, its daring, and its sense of adventure.

As I remember it, the School itself sat near Burton Hall, tucked into a corner of the Loma Linda campus. The building didn't look extraordinary from the outside, but the atmosphere around it did. Tropical plants surrounded the area, giving it the feeling of a living laboratory. When our class went on a field trip there, I remember feeling like we had stepped out of Southern California and into another world.

Inside, the school felt part laboratory, part museum. There were specimens of fish and reptiles, rows of jars with strange contents, and, most unforgettable of all, the shrunken heads. Those left a lasting impression on me as a kid. The story was that Halstead had studied the tribes of South America who practiced the art of shrinking heads. While most people would shudder at the thought, he asked a scientist's question: if you can shrink a head, could the same process be adapted to shrink cancer tumors? To my young mind, that sounded like genius. It was just like him to take something macabre and flip it into a medical possibility.

The School was meant to be a place of serious study, but it carried an aura of adventure. Even as children, walking through its halls gave us the sense that something important, and maybe even world-changing, was happening there.

My friendship with Dr. Halstead's son Larry gave me a more personal window into his world. The Halsteads lived in Grand Terrace, and their home was a gathering spot. They were popular, and their swimming pool made them even more so. But the pool wasn't what fascinated me most. It was the little retreat behind the house where Dr. Halstead worked.

The path back to his office felt like walking into a tropical jungle. Ponds with fish glistened in the sun. Wooden bridges arched across narrow waterways. Exotic plants lined the trail, thick enough to make you forget you were still in Southern California. Disneyland had its Jungle Cruise, but this was the real thing, and it felt even more magical.

Photo Credit: brucehalstead.blogspot.com

At the end of the path stood his office. If the garden outside felt like a jungle, the inside was a library exploded. Books covered every surface — stacked on desks, piled high on file cabinets, crammed onto shelves that strained under their weight. To this day, I don't think I've ever seen so many books in one place outside of a public library. But these weren't just for show. Halstead used them constantly, chasing down references, comparing findings, feeding his endless curiosity. It was a place alive with knowledge, and even as a boy, I could sense that.

Even before his medical degree, Halstead had been preparing for this role. He studied zoology at UC Berkeley and trained in ichthyology under Eugene Clark at the Golden Gate Academy of Sciences in San Francisco. By the time he arrived at Loma Linda, he was already an expert in fish. It was no surprise that when he began to dream about medical research, he focused on the ocean. His idea, which he liked to call "Drugs from the Sea," was simple but profound: natural poisons and venoms might hold the keys to developing medicines for human illness.

In the beginning, CME administrators weren't sure the School of Tropical Medicine could ever succeed. Research money was scarce, and they thought scientific investigation was a luxury the school couldn't afford. Halstead proved them wrong. When his first grant proposal was rejected, he didn't give up — he got on a train and went to Washington, D.C., himself. He met with the Navy, who had ships and logistics, and with the NIH, who had money. Against the odds, he came home with both Navy contracts and NIH grants. Almost overnight, the School went from an idea on paper to a serious research center.

The Navy wanted him to study the toxins of marine creatures like the puffer fish, which could kill a man in minutes. The Army soon followed, awarding contracts after their Commandant came to Loma Linda and realized the potential of partnering with a school connected to a worldwide medical mission network. Within a decade, the once-doubted school was respected across Washington and recognized around the world.

Halstead's obsession with poisons reached its peak with his monumental three-volume work, *Poisonous and Venomous Marine Animals*. Twenty years in the making, it became the largest project ever published by the U.S. Government Printing Office. That work made him the world's leading authority in the field and gave Loma Linda an unlikely international reputation for toxicology.

But Halstead's curiosity was never limited to fish. His expeditions into the jungles of South America opened a new path of discovery — medicinal plants. He sought out shamans and tribal healers who had used botanicals for generations. They showed him which plants treated which illnesses, how they were prepared, and how they were administered. He brought back specimens, labeled them, and studied them. Some of his adventures were so vivid that Hollywood took notice; his work with the Jivaro Indians of the Amazon became the inspiration for the film *The Medicine Man*.

Photo Credit: brucehalstead.blogspot.com

In 1958 he founded the World Life Research Institute to expand this botanical work. He was especially drawn to compounds with anticancer properties. One of them was laetrile, derived from apricot pits. Only years later did he discover that his own biological father, Newton Mellars, had been among those who pioneered research into laetrile's cancer-fighting potential. It was a twist of fate that seemed almost too coincidental — but it only deepened Halstead's conviction that nature had hidden cures waiting to be found.

His reach went beyond the Americas. In the early 1950s he collaborated with Soviet scientist Israel Brekhman, who had discovered the health benefits of Siberian ginseng. Halstead was the first to bring Siberian ginseng to the United States and helped popularize the concept of adaptogenic medicine — natural substances that helped the body resist stress. His later book on the subject, *Eleutherococcus Senticosus*, became a landmark in its own right.

In the 1980s, his research carried him to China, where he worked with institutes studying traditional herbal medicine. What struck him was how closely his independently developed formulas matched those used in Chinese tradition. Together they refined these remedies, and in 1987 he received a Certificate of Merit from the Chinese Institute of Radiation Medicine for his work on herbal compounds that could protect against radiation damage. It was the perfect example of his life's mission: blending Western science with the wisdom of traditional medicine to find new ways of fighting disease.

Through all of this, the School of Tropical and Preventive Medicine remained the foundation. It had started as a corner building by Burton Hall, filled with plants, jars of specimens, and shelves of books. But its vision carried it forward. In 1961 it began offering master's degrees, and on September 1, 1964, it officially became the Loma Linda

University School of Public Health — at the time, only the third public health school in California. That transformation was more than just a name change. It was proof that Halstead's work, and the curiosity he inspired, had placed Loma Linda among the select few institutions shaping the future of global health.

Looking back, what stays with me is not only the importance of the work but the personality of the man behind it. I still picture him in one of his flamboyant Hawaiian shirts, leaning over a microscope, suddenly calling out, "Hey, look at this!" to whoever happened to be nearby. He carried that same energy whether he was in Washington chasing grants, in the Amazon studying plants, or right at home in his Grand Terrace office.

For those of us who saw the School in its early days, it will always be tied to Halstead's restless curiosity. It was a place where science and adventure blurred together, where poisons were viewed as potential cures, and where kids like me could walk away dreaming that the world's mysteries might hold the answers to its diseases. For me, it will always be the tropical retreat near Burton Hall, the shrunken heads that fascinated and unnerved me, and the library of books that seemed too vast for one man to master. And at the center of it all stood Dr. Bruce Halstead, the man in the Hawaiian shirt who turned the strange, the dangerous, and the unknown into a lifelong search for answers.

MIKE KUNERT

Chapter 21

Roy Jutzy

Photo Credit: Loma Linda University Digital Archives

I first met Roy Jutzy at a Wedgwood Trio concert hosted at his son and daughter-in-law's house, Ken and Robyn. What struck me immediately was how approachable he was — warm, engaging, and humble. He was easy to talk with and carried himself with a quiet dignity, the kind of presence that doesn't make headlines but leaves an unmistakable mark on everyone nearby.

His story began far from Loma Linda, in Saskatoon, Saskatchewan, where he was born on May 4, 1924. While still an infant his family moved south to the Pacific Northwest, so his earliest memories were not of the Canadian prairies but of the American Northwest. From childhood he absorbed values of faith, perseverance, and service that would stay with him for nearly ninety-four years.

Like many of his generation, World War II shaped his path. In 1943, at nineteen, he entered the U.S. Army Medical Corps as a dental technician. The discipline and sense of duty forged in those years became permanent parts of his character. After the war he returned determined to practice medicine. He studied at Auburn Academy and Walla Walla College, then went on to the College of Medical Evangelists in Southern California, receiving his MD in 1952. That institution later became Loma Linda University, where he would remain closely tied throughout his career.

He began his medical practice in Cle Elum, Washington, running a small family clinic where he treated everyone who came through the door. Before long, he and his wife, Betty, felt called to mission service, and they spent nearly four years in the Philippines. There he became a physician in the truest sense of the word — delivering babies, treating children, performing surgery when needed. Those years sharpened his adaptability and deepened his faith, teaching him humility and reliance on God in ways that never left him.

When he returned to the United States, he pursued specialization. He trained in internal medicine at Los Angeles County General Hospital and then completed a cardiology fellowship at White Memorial Hospital. At the time, cardiology was still a young field, and Loma Linda was ready to take a pioneering role in it.

In 1963 he was asked to lead twelve junior medical students at Riverside General Hospital during the university's transition from Los Angeles to Loma Linda. That group came to be known as the Twelve Apostles, with Dr. Jutzy as their leader. The experiment proved transformative. It showed that Loma Linda could thrive as a clinical center away from Los Angeles and also demonstrated how mentorship could be rooted in encouragement rather than intimidation. His calm demeanor and steady hand gave students confidence and left a lasting impression on both them and the institution.

By 1965 he had joined the cardiology faculty at Loma Linda University. Over time he rose to chief of cardiology (1976–1990) and then chair of medicine (1990–1995). He retired from administration in 1994 and from clinical practice in 1999, leaving behind decades of students and colleagues shaped by his leadership.

One of the most remarkable parts of his career was his work with the Overseas Heart Surgery Team. Partnering with surgeon Ellsworth Wareham, he helped bring open-heart surgery to countries where it had never been attempted. He traveled to places like China, Greece, Mongolia, Saudi Arabia, and Vietnam, often going ahead of the surgeons to evaluate conditions, connect with local doctors, and make sure everything was ready. Dr. Wareham and others regarded him as a physician's physician — the kind of doctor specialists turned to for judgment and assurance. Wherever he went, he combined skill with humility and faith in a way that carried Loma Linda's mission across cultures.

At home he served as chief of cardiology at the Jerry L. Pettis Veterans Administration Medical Center in Loma Linda. His expertise was also sought internationally, and he advised groups as varied as the U.S. Department of Health, Education, and Welfare in Washington, D.C.; the Saudi Ministry of Defense; the All-Union Cardiac Center in Moscow; and the Ministry of Health in Kabul. His influence stretched from local patients in San Bernardino County to physicians across the world.

He was also a contributor to the medical literature. His work on pacing and pacemakers wasn't the kind that grabbed headlines, but it advanced tools that cardiologists relied on to keep hearts beating. It was typical of him — not flashy, but deeply impactful.

Recognition followed over the years. In 1976, both Walla Walla College and Loma Linda honored him, one as Alumnus of the Year and the other for clinical research. Later he was named Honored Alumnus (1993), received Alumnus of the Year again (2001), and was chosen as Auburn Academy's Distinguished Alumnus that same year. Loma Linda also presented him with its Distinguished Service Award in 1998. He served as president of several organizations, including the Alumni Association and the Walter E. Macpherson Society, yet what people remembered most was not the titles but the way he treated those around him.

Colleagues recalled a man who never raised his voice but still commanded respect. Students remembered his patience and encouragement. Patients remembered the warmth of his presence and his attentiveness.

Family was always central. He and Betty raised five children, and their son Kenneth followed him into cardiology at Loma Linda, specializing in interventional and structural heart disease. Today the Roy and Kenneth Jutzy Endowed Chair in Cardiology honors the family's ongoing influence on the institution.

He retired fully in 1999 and spent his later years in Loma Linda with Betty until her passing in 2013. He lived on until January 4, 2018, when he died at ninety-three. Those who gathered to remember him spoke less about his awards and more about his humor, humility, and steady presence through decades of change.

His life offers several lessons worth keeping. He placed service ahead of self — whether in a mission clinic in the Philippines, a teaching ward in Riverside, or a hospital in Beijing. He believed teaching was as important as treating and that his greatest legacy would be the students who carried his influence forward. His faith was not separate from his medical career but at the heart of it.

Dr. Jutzy's story is, in many ways, the story of Loma Linda itself. It is the story of a young medical school growing into a global institution, of a community carrying its mission worldwide, and of one physician who embodied compassion, service, and faith. He bridged the era from the postwar College of Medical Evangelists to the modern Loma Linda University known around the world.

When I think back to meeting him at his son's home that evening, what comes to mind is not his positions or honors but the warmth of his handshake, the sparkle in his eye, and the feeling that I was in the company of someone who had lived fully and given generously. His life was a testimony to what it means to truly remember Loma Linda by the way one lives it every day.

Chapter 22
Backstory of Loma Linda Community Hospital

By Patti and Jenny Cotton

Photo Credit: Patti and Jenny Cotton

There is no way to tell the story of Loma Linda without telling the story of the Cotton family. Their roots stretched back to Depression-era Massachusetts, where Harold and Dorothy Cotton built a family business of care and grit. Dorothy, a registered nurse, ran nursing homes that offered dignity to the elderly at a time when too many were consigned to asylums. Harold, her husband, was a man who never finished school beyond the fifth or sixth grade—depending on which family storyteller you believed. Yet, with little formal education, he became an inventor, ran welding schools, and during the war years earned Navy commendations for flawless shipyard steelwork. He bought foreclosed mansions during the Depression with cash from his payroll pocket and turned them into homes for the aged. For him and Dorothy, care was business, and business was care.

That legacy carried west when their son, Daniel Cotton, came to California. By 1966, Dan was a professor of religion at La Sierra University, and his wife—a gifted gospel singer—needed the freedom to pursue her calling. On his 35th birthday, he opened Heritage Gardens, a unique retirement and convalescent facility in Loma Linda. Heritage Gardens let couples stay together even if one required medical care and the other did not. It was family by design.

The atmosphere at Heritage Gardens was unlike anything else in the area. Each Friday evening, the Cotton family joined residents for vespers. Retired missionaries told stories of faraway lands, and the children learned that service was a way of life. Patti and Jenny grew up feeding patients, folding laundry, and doing secretarial work. Some days they were washing diapers; other days they were answering phones. To them, the nursing home was an extension of their living room.

Even the landscape reflected symbolism. Olive trees dotted the grounds, and every harvest season neighbors came by to pick and cure them. Dan liked the idea that the olive leaf stood for healing, and he deliberately wove symbols like that into the atmosphere. Heritage Gardens was a place of both care and meaning, where the physical and the spiritual seemed woven together.

But before long, the needs of the town outgrew Heritage Gardens. The university hospital loomed nearby, but many in the community yearned for something less institutional, more personal. Administrators at Loma Linda University themselves saw the need for more beds, for a facility that felt like part of the neighborhood rather than just a training ground for students. They turned to Dan Cotton. He said yes.

That yes set off nearly a decade of obstacles.

First came the hearings—29 public hearings before approval finally came. Neighbors lined up at the microphone to object. Some said traffic would be unbearable. Others claimed their dogs would be disturbed by ambulance sirens, though the university hospital a quarter-mile away was already filled with them. Some whispered fears about competition with the university. Others simply feared change.

The opposition wore on the Cotton family. At home, stress was constant. Dan and his wife often sat at the kitchen table late into the night, reviewing plans and wondering how long they could endure. Their daughters recall the household being filled with anxiety, and yet, the sense of mission never left. There was bewilderment, too: why would neighbors accept the idea of a large convalescent home but not a hospital? Why was one form of care welcome and the other fought tooth and nail?

The fight grew bitter. At one point, reporters credited Harold Cotton, the patriarch, with being behind the hospital plan. It was wrong. This was Dan's initiative, born of his own conviction, but in newsprint the misattribution stung. For Dan, the hospital was a point of personal pride—something he alone had built, though his father's advice was never far away.

Through it all, Dan held fast to an old-fashioned ethic: a handshake was a contract. He kept his word, even when others did not. That was perhaps the deepest wound of all—not the hearings, not the insults, not the delays—but learning that some of his own brethren in Loma Linda business and church life did not share his sense of honor. Where Dan sought service, others sought prestige and power.

Still, he pressed on. Quietly, supporters encouraged him. Physicians came to him privately, promising their backing once the doors opened. Ordinary townspeople told him to keep going. But in public, the opposition was loud, and the encouragement whispered.

At last, in February 1971, the Loma Linda Bulletin announced the decision: the hospital could be built. Yet even then, compromises were forced. The plan for a four-story hospital was cut down to two, then finally to one, after neighbors complained it would block their views of the mountains. Ironically, just years later, the university would erect multi-story complexes that dwarfed anything Cotton had proposed. But by then, the fight was over.

Construction began across the street from Heritage Gardens. The Cottons remember it not just as steel and concrete but as a family adventure. They drove to Tijuana to haul back giant wrought-iron chandeliers, ten feet wide, to hang in the new lobby. They watched their father switch between his "business uniform"—a dark suit and tie—and his "work uniform" of hard hat and rolled-up sleeves. The hospital was, in every sense, his creation.

Dan was, at heart, a man of faith. He had once been a pastor, then a professor of theology, and he never lost the conviction that his work was ministry. Business was just another pulpit. To him, every employee was valuable, every patient a child of God. He did not believe in ministering only from behind a lectern. He believed you could minister by the way you treated people, by the opportunities you created, by the atmosphere of dignity you built into your work.

When the hospital opened, it did so with fanfare worthy of Hollywood. A helicopter landed on the lawn, carrying Mayor Doug Welber, Director of Nursing Rosalie Mitchell, and Dan Cotton himself. Ribbons were cut, hands were shaken, and the hospital was christened Loma Linda Community Hospital. It was full from day one, bustling with patients and grateful physicians who could finally extend their practices.

The grand entrance, with its helicopter and ribbon, bore the stamp of Dan's wife, who loved a splash of drama. Dan was reserved by nature, more comfortable in the background. But she knew the importance of making a moment memorable, and the opening day remains fixed in memory.

For the community, it meant more than beds. It meant jobs—often created by Dan himself when none existed. It meant dignity, because every employee and every patient mattered. To this day, Patti and Jenny still meet people who stop them and say, "Are you Dan Cotton's daughter?" and then tell of how he quietly helped them, gave them work, or offered a kindness that changed their lives.

In time, the hospital passed to Loma Linda University and became today's East Campus. Dan did not profit heavily; he had once even offered to donate it outright. Eventually he sold it, recovering little more than the sweat equity of years of struggle. But the story does not end with the sale. The true story of Loma Linda Community Hospital is not brick and mortar, not ribbon-cuttings or zoning battles. It is the story of a man with faith and tenacity, who carried forward his parents' legacy of care, and built something his community both fought and desperately needed.

It was born in struggle, raised in opposition, and matured into a place of healing. That is the real story of Loma Linda Community Hospital.

Chapter 23

Wall of Water

By: Genie Nelson Sample

Photo Credit: Genie Nelson Sample

My dad, Stan Nelson, built our house in the shadow of the original hospital on the hill with his own hands. From the front, it looked like any other home, a modest and well-kept place in a quiet neighborhood. But those who stepped inside knew it was something special. It wasn't just a house—it was a masterpiece, a labor of love, and a place filled with wonder. It had a wall of water.

Dad was never one to do things the easy way. He always saw the world differently, with an inventor's eye and a craftsman's hands. The idea for the pool came from a trip to Marineland. He watched the massive aquarium windows in awe, fascinated by how they created an entirely new way to experience water. And just like that, he decided—he was going to bring that magic home.

It was no small task. A big walnut tree had to be removed to make room for the basement expansion, and the design had to be perfect. Dad was meticulous, making sure the pool wall featured a massive glass panel—an underwater window that would allow us to see straight into the shimmering blue. When it was finished, it was breathtaking. At night, when the pool lights came on, the water seemed to glow, casting rippling patterns on the walls. I'd sit there for hours, mesmerized by it.

Of course, it didn't take long for word to spread. The pool became the place to be, a gathering spot for family, friends, and neighbors. Saturday nights turned into legendary parties, with laughter and splashes echoing through the house. Sometimes, we'd just sit in the basement, watching our guests swim by like fish in an enormous tank. Whole classes would gather for celebrations, and it wasn't unusual to see a dozen kids all diving in at once, their excited chatter filling the air. My dad loved it. He took so much pride in seeing people enjoy what he built.

One night, we had an unexpected visitor. There was a knock at the front door, and while my mom answered it, Dad heard something in the back. He moved quickly, stepping into the primary bedroom to find a young man digging through his old Horlicks malted milk container filled with change. Without hesitation, Dad grabbed him and marched him straight to the pool. One quick toss, and the would-be thief learned a lesson he wouldn't soon forget. He never came back.

The pool saw a lot of firsts. It was where my brother Ken got his first taste of diving, where my cousins and I spent entire summers racing from one end to the other. There was even a little hearth in the basement, just beneath the great window, where my husband and I sat on our wedding night, unwrapping gifts while our family gathered around us. I can still picture the mound of wrapping paper around us, my dad smiling from his chair, watching us take in the start of our new life together.

And then there was my dad's wildest idea—one that, looking back, should have terrified us all. At my husband's 40th birthday luau, he decided it would be fun to jump into the pool from the top of our chimney. It was ridiculous, but somehow, he convinced a few brave souls to climb the ladder he had set up. One by one, they leaped, plunging into the glowing blue water below. That was just Dad—always pushing limits, always making things exciting. He was a risk-taker, but not reckless. He made sure the pool was deep enough, the angles were just right. If anything, he probably enjoyed the engineering of the stunt more than the jump itself.

And that was the thing about Dad—he was always dreaming up new ways to make life more exciting. He didn't just build pools; he built playgrounds, gathering places, experiences. He built the Eisenhower High School pool, a project that brought him a lot of pride. But none of those projects were quite as personal as the one in our backyard. That was his legacy, his passion poured into concrete and water.

The house itself was never stagnant. It evolved with us, from hardwood floors to carpeting, from a small home to a family landmark. It was more than a place to live; it was where we grew up, where we celebrated, and where we learned to dream. I can still remember lying in my bed as a child, listening to the sounds of the parties happening outside, wishing I were just a few years older so I could be out there too.

But time moves on, and eventually, the house was sold. The new owners made changes, and the pool—the centerpiece of my childhood—was filled in. The great glass window disappeared. I joke that maybe they turned it into an ant farm, but the truth is, I don't know what happened to it. Maybe they just couldn't appreciate what it had been.

Even though the pool is gone, and the house belongs to someone else, the memories remain. I can still hear the echoes of laughter, still see the shimmering water through that wall of glass. My dad built something extraordinary, something that no one who ever saw it could forget. And while the physical space may have changed, what he created will always live on in my heart.

Because my dad, Stan Nelson, didn't just build a pool—he built a world of magic, wonder, and love.

Chapter 24

The Slater Family

There's a small house in Loma Linda that lives quietly in my memory, though I haven't seen it in decades. It sat on a regular street in a regular neighborhood, nothing especially grand or striking about it. But it's stayed with me all these years, because it was the home of my best friend when I was a kid—and more importantly, the home of his father, Jim.

This story isn't really about childhood games or the adventures we had running around that neighborhood. It's about Jim—Dr. James M. Slater—a man who began with humble roots and went on to change the way cancer is treated around the world. And while his professional accomplishments are known by many, what I carry with me is something more personal: the quiet kindness, the persistence, and the sharp mind of a man who changed lives in more ways than one.

Jim was born in 1929 in Salt Lake City. His parents were educated—his father held a degree, and his mother was a schoolteacher, which, for that time, was something to be proud of. Education wasn't just important in their household; it was expected, nurtured. Jim soaked it up. In third grade, he had a teacher named Miss Evans who liked to read stories about scientists and inventors. That classroom, filled with wooden desks and dusty chalkboards, is where the first sparks of curiosity and possibility were lit. He began to imagine doing something important, something lasting.

By the age of fourteen, Jim was already working for the Forest Service. He didn't mind getting his hands dirty—he never did. In fact, some of the jobs he held through his teenage years and early adulthood might surprise you: mechanic, miner, vacuum cleaner repairman. Each one gave him a new way of looking at the world, a fresh angle, a skill he'd carry forward. He never stopped learning. That was one of the things I always admired most about him.

He graduated from high school and earned a degree in physics from the University of Utah in 1955. It was a good time to be a physicist, and Jim could have taken his career in any number of directions. But he had a young family to think about, and like a lot of smart, practical people, he opted for something stable. He moved to California and took a job teaching math at Fontana Junior High.

That could've been the whole story. A smart man, a steady job, raising a family in postwar Southern California. But there was something in Jim that wouldn't settle. A neighbor—a friend, the kind of friend who sees something in you that maybe you haven't quite seen yourself—suggested he think about going to medical school. Not just any school, but Loma Linda University, a place known for thinking a little bigger about healthcare. Jim listened. And then, he applied.

He was accepted, and everything changed.

This was the time I really got to know the Slaters. I spent so many afternoons at their house, hanging around with Jimmy—Jim's son—who was one of my closest friends. They were a close-knit family, kind and a little methodical in a charming way. All the kids had names starting with "J": Jimmy, Julie, Jan, Jerry, Jonny. Even JoAnn, Jim's wife. The following very grainy images are taken from my grandmother's home movie:

From left to right- Me, Jimmy, Jerry, Jan, Julie. (not pictured, Jonny)

Shirtless Med Student Jim Slater taking a short break from studying by watering the lawn. 12 years later he was known as

James M. Slater, MD, and was recruited to develop a radiation oncology program at Loma Linda University Medical Center (LLUMC).

I remember thinking, even as a kid, that there was something orderly about it, like Jim brought the same thoughtfulness to parenting that he brought to everything else. They were warm, welcoming people.

In 1963, Jim graduated from medical school. The family moved away after that—first to Utah, then Los Angeles—so he could complete his residency. And that's when the different parts of his life—his past as a physicist, his training in medicine, his relentless curiosity—began to intertwine.

He earned a fellowship at MD Anderson in Texas, one of the top cancer treatment centers in the world. There, he saw firsthand the toll conventional radiation therapy took on patients. He watched them grow so weak they had to pause their treatments to recover, knowing full well the cancer didn't pause in return. He knew enough physics to realize something wasn't right. There had to be a better way.

That's when Jim began thinking seriously about proton therapy—about using charged particles to target cancer with laser-like precision, sparing healthy tissue in the process. It wasn't just a theory; it was a vision. One that, if realized, could help people heal without the suffering that so often came with the cure.

He returned to Loma Linda in 1970 and didn't waste any time. He developed a CT-based, computer-assisted treatment system—cutting-edge at the time—and earned international awards. But it was only the beginning. He believed protons were the answer. And when Jim believed something, he didn't stop.

The problem was, no one else believed it. Every company he approached turned him down. The technology was too complex, too expensive, too untested. But Jim was persistent. Eventually, he found a company near Chicago willing to take a chance. They had an accelerator nearly four miles long, and they thought they could scale it down for medical use.

Of course, there was a catch. Jim had to convince the board at Loma Linda University to approve the project. Then he had to raise $25 million to build it. And proton therapy had never even been used in a hospital before. He was pitching something no one had seen, something they couldn't yet imagine. It was a leap of faith.

He didn't do it alone. With the help of Congressman Jerry Lewis and others who believed in him, the funding came together. The final cost ended up being closer to $100 million, and the machine itself—the 400-ton cyclotron—required a massive underground facility. It could generate 250 million electron volts. Numbers that sound like science fiction. But they were real.

In 1991, the world's first hospital-based proton treatment center opened at Loma Linda. And when they turned the machine on, it worked exactly as Jim had said it would. Proton beams struck tumors with precision, leaving healthy tissues untouched. Side effects dropped dramatically. Patients recovered faster. And something incredible had happened—a new era of cancer treatment had begun.

Today, more than 1,200 proton therapy centers exist around the world. That's Jim's legacy. But even more amazing is that the original cyclotron at Loma Linda still runs. Still treats patients. It's been upgraded over the years, maintained with care, and it performs better now than when it was first installed over thirty years ago. That kind of longevity doesn't happen by accident.

I never thought I'd be one of those patients. But two and a half years ago, I was diagnosed with prostate cancer. My PSA was 6.1. I sat with the news in that stunned silence people talk about, then made the call to Loma Linda. I knew where I wanted to go. I had known for sixty-five years.

The treatment was easier than I could've imagined. There was no pain, hardly any side effects. I thought about Jim every day I walked through those doors. About his stubborn belief that things could be better. About all the times people told him it couldn't be done. And now, here I was—one life among thousands—walking through the center he built, receiving the care he made possible.

As of my last checkup, my PSA is 0.2. I'm cancer-free. That house I used to walk to as a kid—the one where I'd sit on the floor with Jimmy and trade stories—gave me something I never expected: it gave me more time. Jim Slater saved my life. I don't say that lightly.

But more than that, he gave hope to so many. Thousands of people walk into proton therapy centers around the world, not knowing the name Jim Slater, not realizing the sacrifices, the persistence, the intellect that made it all possible. But that's okay. Jim didn't do it for recognition. He did it because he saw a better way and refused to let it stay an idea.

He passed away in 2014, but his legacy is alive and well. The James M. Slater Proton Treatment and Research Center is more than just a name on a building. It's a symbol of what can happen when one person refuses to give up on a good idea. It's a place of healing, of science and compassion working side by side.

When I look back now, I don't just see the man who helped pioneer a medical breakthrough. I see the father of my friend. The quiet man who sat at the dinner table while we ran around the house. The man who built something that has outlived him and will continue to help people long after the rest of us are gone.

We never know how the people we meet in childhood will shape our lives. But in Jim's case, I got to witness something rare—a life that changed the world, not through flash or fame, but through thought, patience, and a refusal to accept "no."

That's the real story of Dr. James M. Slater. Not just the machines or the physics or the hospital wings. But the belief that one life can ripple outward and touch thousands more. And in his case, it did—one proton at a time.

Footnote: Linked through this QR code is a rare treasure — an 8mm film my grandmother shot of the Slater family in the mid-1950s. I digitized it and placed it on YouTube so it would endure. One of the brothers has said his mother told him that this is the only moving image of them as a young family.

Chapter 25

Van Unger

Gas and Gavel

Photo Credit: Loma Linda Area parks & Historical Society

Every town has its characters, the people who manage to stand just a little taller than everyone else, even if they weren't especially tall. For me, one of those larger-than-life figures was Judge Van E. Unger. He wasn't just a name in the paper or a man behind a bench. He was the guy who filled your gas tank, gave out stern lectures in his courtroom, built his own adobe house, and, at least in my childhood imagination, had the power to toss me into jail at any moment.

My first memories of him go back to his service station at the corner of Central and San Mateo. It was one of those places that felt like the hub of the world, at least for our small part of the Inland Empire. People came not only to fuel up their cars, but also to trade stories, grab a cold soda, and catch up on neighborhood news. I remember being four or five years old, sitting in my grandfather's truck as we pulled in for gas. My grandfather leaned down and told me, "Be nice to him. He can put you in jail." That little aside was apparently meant as a joke, and it worked well enough for the grown-ups, because he and the judge got a good laugh out of it. But to me, it was dead serious.

From then on, my relationship with Judge Unger was defined by sheer terror. Every time I saw him, I straightened up like I was already in court. No smart remarks, no fidgeting, no backtalk. I figured if I so much as sneezed wrong, I'd wind up behind bars in a striped suit with a tin cup, like the cartoon convicts I saw in the Sunday funnies. The thing about childhood fears is that sometimes the world conspires to confirm them. One day, while Judge Unger was putting new tires on my grandfather's truck, I went exploring. I wandered into his chambers—his little courtroom attached to the shop—and there he was in full judge mode. He was scolding a defendant with the kind of voice that could peel paint. That was it. My fate was sealed. Clearly this man could, and would, toss a fellow in jail without so much as a sandwich to go. I stood there listening, my eyes wide as hubcaps, certain that if I even breathed too loud, I'd be next.

Photo Credit: Loma Linda Area parks & Historical Society

Of course, Judge Unger wasn't just the bogeyman of my imagination. He was the real deal: elected Justice of the Peace for San Bernardino County's Mission Township in 1946, a role he would hold for thirty years. That's three decades of traffic citations, small claims, and neighborhood squabbles passing under his gavel. By the time he retired in 1976, he was an institution. The city even gave him a formal send-off, complete with the mayor presiding, which tells you just how well-regarded he was. But he wasn't all about stern lectures and stiff penalties. As I grew older, I learned he had another side—one that had nothing to do with the law and everything to do with community.

Judge Unger was a faithful member of Campus Hill Seventh-day Adventist Church in Loma Linda. He helped organize the first Pathfinder Club in town, giving kids a place to learn, camp, and grow. Imagine my surprise when I realized the man I'd spent half my life terrified of was also leading children's nature hikes, teaching knot-tying, and probably roasting marshmallows over a campfire. It was like learning that Darth Vader also taught Cub Scouts on the weekends.

And he didn't stop there. Alongside Stanley Nelson, he spearheaded a mission project in Valle de la Trinidad, Mexico, during the early 1960s. What started as a youth outreach blossomed into a medical and dental clinic, a school, a model farm, and even two churches. It was hard to reconcile this with the image of the man in black robes chewing out some poor defendant in his courtroom. Yet there it was: a man of discipline, yes, but also of vision and compassion. That same hands-on spirit showed up closer to home too. He built his own adobe house—brick by brick. In a world where most of us would rather hire a contractor, Judge Unger rolled up his sleeves and did it himself. There's something wonderfully stubborn and old-fashioned about that.

Photo Credit: Loma Linda Area parks & Historical Society

My mother and his daughter Marjorie were best friends as teenagers, which gave me another angle on the Unger household. Where I saw a man who could lock you up for jaywalking, she saw her friend's dad—the guy who grilled dinner, asked about homework, and probably grumbled if the lawn wasn't mowed straight. He and his first wife, Agnes, raised their family in Loma Linda, and after she passed away in 1997, he remarried Dr. Verna Towsley. Together, Van and Verna supported Loma Linda University, showing up on the School of Dentistry's honor roll of donors. That was the kind of legacy he built—not just in brick and mortar, but in relationships.

After his long career, Judge Unger retired to a ranch in Mentone. That's where our paths crossed again, this time as neighbors. He was upstream from me on the Zanja, just east of Ward Way. By then, I wasn't a scared little kid anymore. I could appreciate him for what he really was: a steady, reliable presence, a neighbor with stories, and a man who had lived enough for two lifetimes. We'd talk as neighbors do—about the water, about crops, about whatever was going on in town. I still couldn't shake a little of that childhood awe, but the fear was gone. Now I saw him as part of the fabric of the community, not the long arm of the law.

Photo Credit: Loma Linda Area parks & Historical Society

When you look at Judge Unger's full story, it's hard not to be impressed. Born in Missouri in 1909. Raised in Loma Linda by his grandparents after family tragedy. Gas station owner. Justice of the Peace for thirty years. Pathfinder leader. Mission organizer in Mexico. Builder of adobe homes. Rancher in Mentone. Church elder. Family man. He lived to the age of ninety-six, passing away in 2006. He left behind children, grandchildren, great-grandchildren, and countless neighbors with stories like mine—some funny, some serious, all memorable.

Looking back, I can't help but laugh at how seriously I took my grandfather's warning. "Be nice to him. He can put you in jail." That single sentence launched years of perfect posture and quiet obedience on my part. I suppose it didn't do me any harm. If anything, it gave me a deep respect for authority figures—and maybe kept me out of a little trouble. But more than that, it gave me a story. And stories are what knit together the life of a town like Loma Linda. Judge Unger was part of ours: sometimes feared, often admired, and in the end, fondly remembered. Because sometimes the people who scare you most as a kid turn out to be the ones who make the best neighbors.

Chapter 26

Dr. Ellsworth Wareham and the Heart Team

How many people celebrate their 100th birthday by mowing their lawn? I only know of one. I first met Dr. Ellsworth Wareham at his home in Oak Glen sometime in the mid-1970s. He was probably in his fifties then. I had been introduced by a mutual friend, Don Morris, who was helping put up a new building for him. Wareham had this idea of building an English cottage, right down to the thatched roof. It was unusual, maybe even a little eccentric, but what struck me most was the man himself. He was warm, engaging, and easy to talk with. There was no hint of arrogance about him. Here was a man who had saved lives all over the world, and yet he stood there smiling and talking about his dream cottage as if we were old friends.

By then, of course, Wareham was already a legend in medicine. He had been born in 1914 in Texas, the son of a Seventh-day Adventist farming family that later moved to Alberta, Canada during the Depression. Times were hard. Wheat sold for thirty cents a bushel, oats for six or seven. Animals were worth almost nothing. He later recalled that none of his classmates ever earned a college degree, but somehow the conviction came upon him, as strong as hunger, that he had to be a doctor. There was no other option.

He scraped his way into school, selling Adventist books door-to-door to help pay his way. After attending Canadian Junior College (now Burman University), he pushed through additional coursework to make up for the science credits he lacked. He went on to medical school at what was then the College of Medical Evangelists — the school that would later become Loma Linda University. He graduated in 1942, served as a surgeon near the end of World War II, and trained in Los Angeles, New York, and Minneapolis before returning to Loma Linda. Along the way, he met Barbara, a nurse who became his wife in 1950. Together they raised five children.

At Loma Linda, Wareham quickly became known as a steady hand and a calming presence. The new field of open-heart surgery was risky and stressful. Surgeries sometimes stretched on for hours, and a single mistake could mean the difference between life and death. But Wareham was never rattled. His colleague, cardiologist Joan Coggin, once said she never saw him riled, no matter what went wrong. If a machine malfunctioned or the patient's blood supply ran low, he would calmly say, "Well, we'll just have to do this and this," always in a moderate tone. That steadiness made him not just a surgeon but a leader.

The story of the Heart Team, which would carry Loma Linda's name around the world, began in a very simple way. In the early 1960s, Loma Linda still didn't have all the equipment it needed, so once a week Wareham and Coggin drove to Los Angeles County General Hospital to do surgeries. They packed up the bulky heart-lung machine, loaded it into Wareham's station wagon, and hauled it across town. That routine sparked the idea: if they could move it across Los Angeles, why not across the world?

The opportunity came in 1963, with a little help from Washington. At the time, President John F. Kennedy's administration was looking for ways to improve America's image abroad. Vice President Lyndon Johnson had visited Pakistan, and after a Pakistani girl was brought to Los Angeles for heart surgery, Johnson's office asked if Loma Linda's team might go to Karachi. Wareham's response was straightforward: if they would cover the travel and shipping costs, he and his team would go. Six of them packed up the heart-lung machine and supplies, shipped them halfway around the world, and got to work.

Those early surgeries in Karachi weren't easy. Local cultural beliefs made it difficult to find blood donors. In Pakistan at that time, many Muslims equated giving blood with sacrificial bloodletting. Wareham and his team worked around it by drawing on American military personnel from the embassy. They even figured out how to reuse the same blood in the morning and afternoon if the types matched — something that had never been tried before. In just 22 operating days they performed 44 surgeries, saw 300 patients, and trained local doctors who would go on to found the Pakistan Heart Institute.

That first mission was a success, and it proved the concept. From then on, the Loma Linda University Overseas Heart Surgery Team — simply called the Heart Team — became a traveling lifeline. They carried out surgeries in India, Thailand, Taiwan, Greece, Vietnam, Saudi Arabia, Hong Kong, Kenya, Zimbabwe, China, Chile, North Korea, and Nepal. Wherever they went, they either initiated or upgraded heart surgery programs.

The stories from those trips could fill a book on their own. In Bangkok, the blood used to prime the machine was too warm, so the whole operation had to be paused, the machine cleaned out, and the process restarted. Wareham didn't flinch. In Vietnam, the team performed sixty open-heart surgeries at Saigon Adventist Hospital in just over a month while war was still raging. In Saudi Arabia in 1976, they carried out the very first open-heart operation in the kingdom, completing 86 surgeries in four months with patients flown in by the Royal Saudi Air Force.

Through all of this, Wareham remained unflappable. Joan Coggin later said that his calm spirit under pressure was as important as his skill. She meant it. Surgeons often carry their personalities into the operating room, but with Wareham the tone was always steady, never frantic.

By the time he retired from the operating table in his mid-nineties, Wareham had performed more than 12,000 operations. Even in his later years he continued to assist younger surgeons, and at 100 years old he was still driving, gardening, mowing his own lawn, and living in the two-story home he shared with Barbara. When people asked Barbara whether she thought he should retire, she just laughed and said, "Leave him alone. He's happy."

In his later years, Wareham became almost as famous for his longevity as for his surgical career. He was held up as a quintessential "Blue Zone" resident — someone who lived in one of the healthiest parts of the world. He ate a vegan diet, exercised, had a sense of humor, and placed his faith in God at the center of his life. Asked by Dr. Mehmet Oz about worry, Wareham replied, "If He's in charge of my life, why sit around and worry? He takes care of the universe, He can certainly take care of me."

He mentored younger surgeons, including Leonard Bailey, who would go on to perform the world's first infant heart transplant. He was honored at his 100th birthday by Loma Linda University with the creation of the Ellsworth E. Wareham Global Service and Education Fund. And when he passed away in December 2018 at the age of 104, people remembered him not just as a surgeon, but as a man who embodied humility, kindness, and faith.

For those of us who lived in and around Loma Linda, his story feels like part of our own. He embodied the values that made the town what it is: faith, service, health, and humanity. He never chased prestige, but prestige found him anyway. He never tried to make himself the story, yet somehow he was always at the center of remarkable stories.

When I think back to that day in Oak Glen, standing beside Don Morris while Wareham talked about his English cottage project, it all makes sense. He wasn't just a great doctor, he was a builder — of structures, of programs, of people, of lives. He built hope. And in doing so, he helped make the name of Loma Linda known around the world, one heartbeat at a time.

Chapter 27

The Vegetable Truck and Other Forgotten Luxuries

People love to gripe about how "the retail experience isn't what it used to be." You hear it all the time. "Nobody wants to go to the store anymore." "Everyone's so lazy—they just get things delivered." They say it like it's a bad thing.

But I remember when getting things delivered wasn't some newfangled concept—it was life. In fact, if you lived in Loma Linda in the 1950s, you could probably survive for months without ever going to a grocery store. Nearly everything came to your door, or was just a short walk away.

This wasn't some urban convenience. This was small-town simplicity at its finest.

Take the vegetable truck, for example.

I don't want to overhype the thing. It was just an old truck. Probably a Chevy one-ton or something close to it. Painted dark green. It had a canvas over the top and sideboards removed to make it easier to reach the boxes inside. But it represented something more than just produce. It was part of a rhythm of life that doesn't exist anymore.

I think the guy who drove it was named Mr. Perkins. I'm not 100% sure, but that name rattles around in the attic of my memory, and it feels right. He would show up in our neighborhood twice a week. Like clockwork. And he'd let everyone know he was there by blasting this weird, unforgettable horn. It wasn't quite a truck horn and not quite a train whistle—it was somewhere in between, like he was trying to summon both farmers and conductors at the same time.

The second he honked, screen doors creaked open up and down the street. Housewives, grandmothers, even the occasional kid on errand duty—we'd all make our way toward that truck like it was the ice cream man, but for zucchini.

Mr. Perkins didn't just buy stuff from wholesalers. From what I remember, he worked directly with local farmers—guys from Yucaipa, Calimesa, maybe even Cherry Valley. Early each morning, while most of us were still trying to drag ourselves out of bed, he'd already be out visiting farms, buying whatever had just been picked. He paid cash, loaded it up, and brought it straight to us.

He knew his stops. I'm sure it took trial and error, but he figured out which blocks were worth his time and which weren't. Our block on San Mateo made the cut. And I'm glad it did. I remember him standing at the back of that truck, holding a peach in his hand, slicing it in half with a little paring knife, and handing me one side. Not the most hygienic process by today's standards, but let me tell you—it was the best peach I ever tasted. And I've tasted a lot of peaches since then. None of them compare.

I also remember he'd lean against the back of the truck like he had all the time in the world. No rush. No quotas. Just standing there, talking with my grandmother about what crops were coming in next week, or how the cucumbers from the week before turned out. He didn't carry a cash register—just a little apron with pockets and a hand scale hooked to the rail. You picked out what you wanted, and he'd weigh it right there.

Mr. Perkins also kept this tiny red Bible on the dash. About the size of a matchbook. I don't know why I remember that, but I do. Maybe it was his good luck charm. Or maybe it was a reminder that what he was doing—feeding a community—was a kind of ministry all its own.

And he wasn't the only one making deliveries.

Our milkman showed up around 4 a.m. every few days, always rattling the metal crate as he swapped out our empties for full bottles of milk, cream, eggs, and butter. Sometimes cheese. No talking. No doorbell. Just the clang of glass on porch and the quiet hum of the truck disappearing into the night. Occasionally, if we forgot to bring the bottles in right away, they'd sit out too long and the cream would rise to the top and push the little cardboard cap off like a champagne cork. That's how fresh it was.

Then there was the Helms Bakery man. Now that guy was a rock star. He'd pull up in a long yellow truck that looked like a cross between a bus and a breadbox, and when you climbed aboard, he'd open one of those big sliding drawers and—no questions asked—hand you a cookie. Every kid in the neighborhood looked forward to the Helms man. We didn't even care about the bread. We were in it for the cookies.

He had more than just bread and cookies, too. There were pies, doughnuts, pastries, and dinner rolls stacked neatly in those magical drawers. You could hear him coming by the distinctive ding of his bell—different than Mr. Perkins' horn, but just as effective. If you heard it, you dropped what you were doing and ran.

There was also an ice cream truck that came by every afternoon, like clockwork. It looked like a chopped-off pickup with a white freezer box mounted in the bed. You could hear its little musical jingle from three blocks away, and if you didn't start running the second you heard it, you'd miss it entirely. There was one kid on our block who always had exact change. We all hated him for that.

And that was just food.

We had the Avon lady who came by every couple of weeks with lipsticks and powders and little catalogs. Tupperware saleswomen who somehow convinced every mother in town that you could never have too many plastic lids. The

Fuller Brush man with his endless collection of hairbrushes, shoe polish, and whatever else he could carry in that magic suitcase. Encyclopedias, World Book or Britannica—you name it, someone knocked on your door and offered to sell it.

Even the pharmacy delivered. If you were sick, the doctor would come to your house, examine you in your own bed, write a prescription, and then the drugstore would send a kid on a bicycle to deliver it before dinner. That's just how things worked. You got sick, you got better, and you never left the house.

Dry cleaners delivered, too. You'd pin a note and a couple of dollars to your clothes, leave them on the porch, and two days later they came back clean and pressed. Nobody stole them. Nobody tampered with them. It was a different world.

And if you needed something you couldn't get locally, you had the Sears catalog. It was like a printed-out Amazon, only heavier and with better illustrations. Everything was in there. Tools, toys, clothes, radios, furniture, even houses you could assemble yourself. You could either mail in your order or call it in, and they'd ship it to you. No credit cards—just cash or check. Sometimes you paid the mailman when he showed up. Sometimes you paid in advance. But it always arrived.

We didn't have UPS, FedEx, or drones. We had faith in the mailman. And it worked.

And here's something I miss most of all: when people knocked on your door trying to sell something, they weren't treated like pests. My grandmother would always greet them with a smile, even if she wasn't buying. She'd thank them for thinking of her, for taking the time to come by. If someone offered to mow the lawn or sweep the porch for fifty cents, she'd usually let them. Not because we couldn't do it ourselves, but because she believed in helping people who were trying to help themselves.

No one panhandled. They worked. Even if it was just for a dollar or two. And people appreciated it. It was a small economy of trust and respect, and it kept the wheels turning.

And what's funny is—after all these years—we're right back where we started.

Today, we've come full circle in a strange way. After decades of glorifying the mall, the strip mall, the megastore—we're back to home delivery. We've got Instacart for groceries, DoorDash for food, Amazon for everything else. The only difference is that now it comes in brown boxes with barcodes instead of green trucks with peaches.

But something's missing.

We lost the personal touch. The familiar face. The guy who gave you a cookie or remembered that your grandma liked nectarines better than plums. Mr. Perkins didn't need a GPS to find our house. He knew where we lived. And when he showed up, it meant more than just vegetables.

It meant someone cared enough to bring you something good.

So yeah, the vegetable truck is gone. The Helms man is gone. The milkman is long retired. But I still remember. And every time I hear someone complain about how "everyone just wants things delivered now," I want to tell them:

We used to do it better.

And if we're smart, maybe we'll find our way back—not just to convenience, but to connection.

Chapter 28

Dr. George

When I think back to the neighborhood where I grew up, there's one house that always comes to mind. It wasn't the fanciest house, or the biggest, or even the prettiest. It sat on the corner where San Marcos meets San Mateo, with a yard that was kept up but never showy, and several orange trees that seemed to stay green and healthy no matter what the season was doing.

I must have walked past it a thousand times, because it sat halfway between my place and the Slaters'. Most of the time, I probably wouldn't have given that house a second thought. Except I knew who lived there.

Her name was Dr. Lyra George. To us she was always Dr. George — not just the kind neighbor down the street, but a real doctor, the kind who came to our house when my grandfather was sick. I was young, and I didn't always understand the details of what was wrong, but I knew enough to know she was the one people trusted when help was needed.

Even outside her role as a doctor, she carried herself with a calm steadiness that made you stop and pay attention. She wasn't tall — barely my height even when I was a kid — but she had a presence. Most of the time, I saw her in her wide-brimmed hat, out among her orange trees.

And those oranges — they were unforgettable.

I'd wave when I walked by. If she waved back, that was my green light to stop. Sometimes I'd stand at the fence while she checked her trees, trimming a branch or reaching for a ripe piece of fruit. Then she'd walk over and talk with me. She asked real questions and actually listened to the answers, something not every grown-up did.

More often than not, she'd hand me one of those oranges. They were the best in the city, as far as I was concerned — heavy in the hand, warm from the sun, and bursting with juice. She'd smile and say, "Better than candy," and she wasn't wrong. I can still remember walking home, peeling one as I went, juice running down my wrist, feeling like I'd just been given something special.

Those orange trees are still there. The house has seen different families come and go, but the trees remain. Every time I pass that corner and see them, I'm reminded of her.

She was more than just the doctor who came when my grandfather was ill. She was a true neighbor. She sat with us when we needed it, without any fuss or show. That was the way she lived her life. Quiet, steady, dependable.

I didn't understand as a child just how far her reach extended. To me, she was Dr. George, the physician who happened to live down the street. But as I grew older, and especially when I began to learn the history of Loma Linda, I realized her story was far larger than I had ever imagined.

Dr. George was a faculty member at the College of Medical Evangelists, what later became Loma Linda University. She was an obstetrician, delivering babies not just in town but in the most remote places in the valley. Many of those trips took her by horseback up into the hills north of Del Rosa, where she visited the Serrano Indians in their adobe homes. And those rides weren't short errands — they took over half a day just to reach the families she was caring for. Over half a day of rough trails, dust, heat, and isolation, just so mothers and infants could have medical care they otherwise would never have received.

She wasn't alone, either. She often brought students with her, using those long trips not only to treat patients but to teach the next generation how to practice medicine with dignity and respect. She didn't dismiss the Serrano traditions; she listened, she learned, and she built trust. That was rare in those days, and it left a mark. Families came to trust her so deeply that many baby girls were named Lyra after her.

That trust never went away. The Serrano people remembered. Their descendants remembered. Over time, the San Manuel Band of Mission Indians became some of the most important partners Loma Linda University ever had. Out of gratitude for Dr. George and for the faculty and students who carried on her work, the San Manuel Band gave generously to support the medical center. Their donations were not small tokens — they added up to more than $25 million for the new hospital. They have never forgotten what Dr. George did for their families in those early years, and their gifts were a way of saying thank you across the generations.

It's remarkable when you think about it. A woman on horseback, making a half-day trip to deliver a baby in a remote home, ends up shaping the very course of a major medical institution a hundred years later. That's legacy.

And she wasn't the kind to boast about it. She never talked to us about those rides, or the babies, or the students. She didn't need to. She lived it.

Her influence didn't stop with her own generation. The example she set — of serving the overlooked, of listening, of showing up — carried forward. In the late 1960s, a new wave of Loma Linda students looked around and saw another group of people who weren't being cared for: migrant farm workers, laborers, and the young drifters of the counterculture. Following in Dr. George's footsteps, they started free evening clinics. They called it the Social Action Corps, or SAC. Faculty supervised, students did the work, and people who would have gone without care finally had somewhere to turn.

Those little evening clinics grew. Over the years, they became the Social Action Community Health System, with clinics all over the region. By the mid-1990s, they had an entire facility at the old Norton Air Force Base, and even that eventually became too small. In 2015, ground was broken for a massive new 150,000-square-foot facility in downtown San Bernardino. Today, the SAC Health System sees more than 100,000 patients a year, providing not just medical care but dental and mental health, and serving as a training ground for new healthcare professionals.

And here's the beautiful part: when that new center was being built, part of it was named San Manuel Gateway College. That name wasn't chosen lightly. It was chosen because of the gratitude the San Manuel Band carried for Dr. George and for the university that followed her example. Their gift — more than $25 million — wasn't just money. It was recognition. It was thanks. It was a direct line from those half-day horseback rides into the hills to a modern, world-class health and education center.

That gratitude has never faded. For generations now, the San Manuel Band has said, in their own words and in their own way, how much they appreciate what Dr. George did for their people, and how much they appreciate the university she helped shape. They never forgot, and they have made sure the rest of us don't forget either.

So when I walked into that hospital lobby a few years ago, and I saw her picture on the wall, it wasn't just nostalgia. It was revelation. The same woman who once handed me oranges and checked in on my grandfather had also laid down a foundation of trust and service that still shapes the valley today.

That's what makes her legacy so extraordinary. It wasn't one big act. It wasn't one grand gesture. It was years of steady presence — in her neighborhood, in her students' lives, in the adobe homes of the Serrano families. It was oranges and porch steps and half-day rides. It was humility and consistency.

And that's why she looms so large in my memory. Because she showed that greatness doesn't need to announce itself. It can live quietly on the corner of San Marcos and San Mateo, with a wide-brimmed hat and a bag of oranges.

Her story hasn't been forgotten. PBS even produced a documentary about her, telling her story in full. If you'd like to see what made her so remarkable, I've included a QR code at the end of this chapter. Scan it, and you can watch for yourself. You'll understand why a small woman with a calm voice and a yard full of orange trees is remembered with gratitude not just by me, not just by our neighborhood, but by whole generations of families who never stopped appreciating what she did.

Chapter 29

Emenel

There's a particular stretch of Barton Road I can't drive past without slowing down a little—right near that magic spot where Loma Linda, Colton, and San Bernardino all quietly meet. One block from that invisible tri-city handshake stands a sturdy building built into the side of a hill, and for anyone else it might just be another relic from the postwar boom. But to me, it's something more. That building holds a story, one I first heard in bits and pieces from my grandfather, and later filled in thanks to my Aunt Betty.

The man behind that building was Dan Mitchell, a quiet, white-haired gentleman who might've blended into the background if you didn't know better. He was one of my grandfather's closest friends and, more importantly to this story, one of the early believers in something few people were talking about back then—dietary supplements. Today, the supplement industry is worth over $200 billion a year. But when Dan got into it, people still gave you funny looks if you said you were taking vitamins that didn't come with a prescription.

I didn't know much about Dan's early years—where he came from or what drove him toward nutrition—but by the time I came along, he was already known for two things: being the most dedicated supplement taker you'd ever meet, and being thrifty to the bone.

When he built that building in the mid-1940s, he did it with a certain kind of practical genius. He picked that hillside location carefully so almost every room would have a clear view of the San Bernardino Mountains. Those big north-facing windows weren't just for the scenery—they let in all the natural light anyone could need. He figured why pay for electricity if the sun would do the job for free?

My Aunt Betty worked for Dan before she was even old enough to drive. She used to walk to the building every day from their house nearby and pitch in wherever she could. Dan was just getting the food supplement side of his business off the ground. At the time, he also ran a bakery with his son Warren, so the place always smelled like something halfway between vitamins and sourdough. His company was called Emenel. No one seems to remember what the "L" stood for anymore—Mitchell and someone, long gone by the time Betty started working there and certainly before my time. But the name stuck.

Why Dan started a supplement business, we're not entirely sure. What we do know is that he received a good amount of research and encouragement from CME, the institution that would eventually become Loma Linda University. Dan wasn't a loud promoter, but he was a true believer. He took everything he sold and believed every capsule was doing good. Smitty, our local barber, had a theory about that. He used to joke that giving Dan a haircut was like trimming a wire brush. Claimed he had to sharpen his scissors every time.

Dan's products weren't just window dressing. They had names, ingredients, and purposes—long before it was fashionable to put "all natural" on a bottle.

In 1947, D.A. Mitchell Laboratories—what would become Emenel—introduced a product called Prostall. It was designed to help men dealing with prostate issues and was made from a mix of nettles, tomatoes, vitamin E, zinc, and selenium. Decades later, you'll still find those same ingredients in prostate health formulas on pharmacy shelves. Dan wasn't ahead of the curve; he *was* the curve.

That same year, he released Ceroplex, a multivitamin that included 33 vitamins and minerals—and proudly boasted being the first to contain vitamin F. Every bottle came with a chart showing how Ceroplex stacked up against the competition. Spoiler alert: the competition didn't come out looking too great. Smitty once said Dan might've gone overboard on the iron content, but Dan just smiled and said it was "for strength of character."

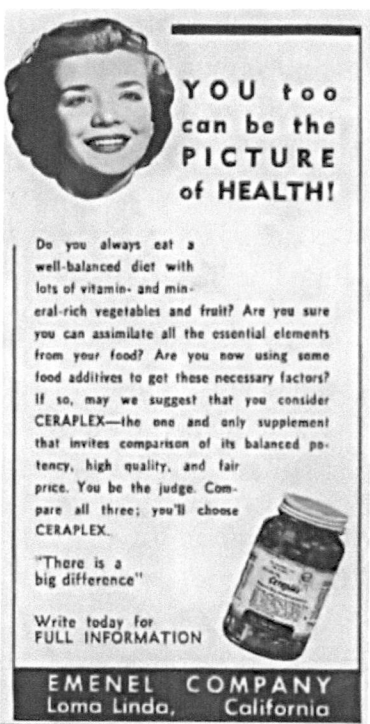

In 1948 came Alfa-Rice, the product Dan would become best known for. Just two ingredients—alfalfa and rice—but packed into a bitter-tasting tablet that was, in Dan's eyes, the perfect supplement. My grandfather swore by them. Ate them like jellybeans for years. He lived to be 99. Make of that what you will.

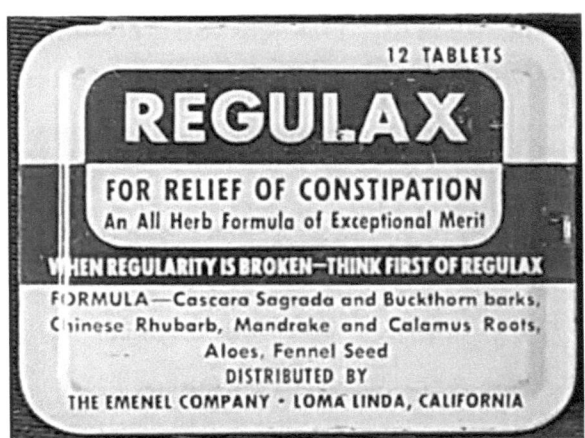

Sofcol came along in 1952, and this one was a little different. It didn't come from natural sources—in fact, its key ingredient, dioctyl sodium sulfosuccinate, started life as a detergent compound patented back in 1937. Someone discovered it made a pretty effective laxative. Dan added fennel seed, put it in a capsule, and marketed it as a gentle remedy for constipation. This was three years before the FDA formally acknowledged it. He was either lucky or just that intuitive. I always wondered how many other detergents were "discovered" the hard way before landing on that one.

By 1953, business was booming, and Dan needed more space. That's when he got wind that Norton Air Force Base had a Quonset hut they were getting rid of. This was no shed—it had been an aircraft hangar, deconstructed and shipped to Norton to be disposed of. Dan saw opportunity. With help from a group of pillmakers and a ragtag crew of academy and med students, he hauled the parts over and managed to reconstruct the whole thing. The structure is still standing, still in use. That tells you everything you need to know about Dan's brand of determination.

People often asked him why he didn't sell the business when the big money came knocking. The offers were there—several big companies tried to buy him out. But Dan wasn't interested. He didn't want to answer to anyone. He liked walking to work from his house next door, liked knowing his products inside and out. Behind his home, he had a curmudgeonly contractor named Reuben Yeager build a series of small rental apartments—eight or ten, I think—as his retirement plan. He paid for the work, I wired the units, and in the process, I got to know Reuben too. He barked like a bulldog but had a soft spot once you got past the grumbling. That project led to a lot more work for me later. Funny how one job can turn into a whole season of your life.

Those apartments gave Dan the retirement income he wanted without having to sell off his business. He kept the pace he liked, stayed in the community he loved, and left a legacy that most people would never recognize unless you knew the story.

And really, that's the thing with Dan Mitchell. He wasn't trying to be a pioneer. He wasn't looking to revolutionize an industry. He just believed in what he was doing. He believed that people needed better health. He believed that good products, made with care and conviction, could help. And he lived that belief quietly, humbly, right here in Loma Linda.

By the time he closed shop in the mid-70s, the industry he helped spark was just beginning to explode. Health food stores were cropping up everywhere. Vitamin shelves were filling. But Dan had already stepped back, content in knowing he'd played his part. I don't think he ever realized just how big it would become. If you told him that the supplement industry would one day bring in more revenue than the GDP of Greece, he probably would've chuckled and said, "Should've trademarked Ceroplex."

The building still stands. Those windows still catch the morning sun just right. And every time I pass by, I think about Dan. I think about Aunt Betty walking to work, about Smitty grumbling over his scissors, about my grandfather crunching on bitter little tablets with a satisfied look on his face. I think about Dan's quiet wisdom, his dry sense of humor, and his rock-solid belief in the value of what he built.

In a world full of noise, Dan was a quiet success. The kind that doesn't get headlines but sticks with the people who knew him. And I count myself lucky to be one of them.

Chapter 30

The LLU UFO

In the middle of the 1960s, Loma Linda University was moving forward as a young institution with a bright future, but there was still a hole in the campus. There was no real gymnasium, no place where the students could gather together under one roof for games, graduations, or even emergencies. The talk around the Board of Councilors kept circling back to the same idea: it was time to build something worthy of a university. The idea that finally took hold was not a simple box of a building but something ambitious. A dome. A geodesic dome, like the ones Buckminster Fuller had made famous, a gleaming futuristic shell that could hold thousands of people and would look like nothing else in the valley.

The dream was ready, but the money wasn't. Then in 1966, Dale Gentry stepped into the story. He was a San Bernardino businessman who owned the California Hotel downtown. The hotel had been grand once, back in the 1920s, but by the 1960s it was past its prime. Gentry could have tried to revive it, or sell it quietly, but instead he did something completely different. On June 30, 1966, he signed the hotel over to Loma Linda University. The very next day the university sold it, and just like that, the project had the three hundred thousand dollars it needed to move forward. Add in support from the Councilors, and the university had its funding. The dome would carry his name in gratitude: the Dale Gentry Gymnasium.

Construction began that fall. For the next year the campus watched as aluminum panels climbed into the sky above Stewart Street. It was billed as the largest aluminum geodesic dome gymnasium in the United States, bigger even than the earlier dome at the National Orange Show. The new gym would cover eighteen thousand square feet of floor space, with a basketball court that could convert into two volleyball courts, folding bleachers, and a three-sided balcony. It could seat 2,800 people, and it was ready by early 1968.

The sight of it was unforgettable. At the same time the Anderson Street Overpass was completed, and every driver cresting the bridge got the same view: a giant silver dome, gleaming in the California sunlight, looking like it had just landed from outer space. Almost immediately it picked up a nickname. People started calling it the LLU UFO. Students teased about it, but they were proud too. There was no mistaking it for anything but modern.

Once the doors opened, the gym was in constant use. Basketball games finally had a home worthy of a crowd, and students roared from the stands. Graduations felt proper, convocations filled the seats, and concerts turned the dome into a music hall. It was pressed into service as more than an arena. When the heavy floods of 1969 forced people out of their homes, cots lined the gym floor and it became a shelter. When Vietnamese refugees arrived in the mid-1970s, they too found temporary housing under the dome. When the church was under renovation, worship services rang out beneath the aluminum canopy.

There were concerts I'll never forget. Van Cliburn himself, the world-famous pianist who had stunned Moscow in 1958, was still touring in the late 1960s and early 1970s, and he performed in the Gentry Gym. His piano rang up into the dome like a bell. Another evening the 1812 Overture was played, complete with cannons, but the cannons had a mind of their own. Instead of firing with the music, they went off whenever they pleased, booming at odd moments while the orchestra carried on, leaving the audience half thrilled and half laughing.

Behind it all was Dale Gentry, and he was a man with a flair for the memorable. He once arranged for the introduction of the "Black Bear of the San Bernardino Mountains," just the sort of showpiece he enjoyed. He loved trains too, but not toy trains. He bought a full-size steam locomotive from Kauai and brought it back to California. For several years he ran it at the National Orange Show, insisting on being the engineer himself. His habit of clipping cars parked too close to the tracks made the organizers nervous, and they finally asked him to take it elsewhere. So he moved it to his ranch in the High Desert, where it became a fixture. These were the kinds of stories people told about Gentry—part entrepreneur, part showman, part philanthropist.

By the end of the 1970s, the Gentry Gym was woven into the fabric of university life. Students remembered their games there, their graduations, the times it sheltered them in crises. Neighbors remembered concerts and convocations. Everyone driving the overpass still saw the UFO, glinting in the sun. All of it had sprung from the decision to turn a declining hotel into a gift.

The dome on Stewart Street was more than steel and aluminum. It was a piece of Loma Linda's story, a reflection of a man who thought in grand gestures and left behind something that outlasted him. It was a building that could house a basketball game one day and a worship service the next, or shelter the community in times of need. It was futuristic and practical, whimsical and serious, all at once. And it still stood there, looking like a spaceship that had landed in Loma Linda and somehow decided to stay.

Chapter 31
The Pool (aka The Plunge)

By Betty Giberson Wieland and Robert Peterson

Photo credit: Loma Linda Area Parks & Historical Society

(Authors note: These are two stories of life at the summer at the pool, separated by approximately two decades. Full disclosure, Betty Giberson Wieland is better known to me as "Aunt Betty".)

By Betty Giberson Wieland

When I think back on my childhood in Loma Linda, one of the brightest spots of every summer was the pool—the plunge, as some called it. It wasn't just a swimming hole. It was the gathering place for kids, families, and friendships that seemed to stretch across every summer afternoon.

I remember the rules being peculiar by today's standards. They separated the boys' hours from the girls' hours. But the whole thing seemed rather pointless because when the boys were in the water, the girls would be just outside the fence—and it was only a regular chain-link fence. So we'd all stand there, talking through the wire mesh, pretending we were separated when really, nothing could keep us apart. Friendships blossomed through those fences. I still laugh, thinking about what that was supposed to accomplish.

There were always stories about kids sneaking into the pool at night. I never did, at least not that I can remember, though I had plenty of friends who swore they did. We all knew who the lifeguard was Reidar Schmidt, and he was as much a part of that pool as the diving board itself. He loved auto racing, and I can still hear the tinny sound of the Indianapolis 500 coming through his radio as we gathered around, dripping wet in our swimsuits, listening as he cheered for his favorite drivers. He never had to rescue anyone that I remember—it was a pretty cushy job—but he was good with the kids. He'd show us flips off the diving board and encouraged us like an older brother. He was more instructor than lifeguard, though it was never official. That was just who he was.

The diving boards themselves were a rite of passage. There was the three-foot board, where we all practiced our flips, and the high dive—a full ten feet. Going off the high dive for the first time was a huge deal. They frowned on anyone climbing back down the ladder once they got scared, so the pressure was real. But once you made that first leap, you felt like you belonged.

Every Friday, they'd drain the pool, and that created its own kind of danger. We'd still swim as the water went lower and lower. Before long, diving off the ten-foot board meant hitting five feet of water, which was a recipe for trouble. That's how I broke a front tooth one summer. I didn't pull up quickly enough, hit my mouth on the bottom, and chipped it clean off. That dumb tooth caused me problems for years afterward, no matter how many times the dentist patched it up.

Photo Credit: Betty Giberson Wieland

The pool was affordable, which mattered in those days. Money was tight for our family, but a yearly pass was something my folks could manage. I think it was around ten dollars, maybe even less. That bought you the whole summer, every single day, and for us kids, it was worth every penny.

Afterward, I would head over to the tennis courts next door—just plain concrete, cracked and worn, but perfect for games. We'd play tennis, roller skate, and when we were daring, play "crack the whip," which sometimes left fingers scraped and bloodied from catching the cracks in the pavement. That whole patch of ground was our world: the ball field, the pool, the tennis courts. No gymnasium, no football field, just the basics. And we made it enough.

We had family days at the pool too, times set aside for parents and kids together. The rest of us schemed to get adopted for an afternoon—"Which family will take me in today?"—so we could swim even if our own folks weren't there. It was all part of the fun.

And then there was the pool house. It was small, cramped, and there were no lockers, just shelves for your clothes. It wasn't fancy, but it was memorable. That's where all the girls learned to shave their legs. A whole generation sitting on benches in swimsuits, nervously dragging razors across skin for the first time. Funny the things that stick with you.

We played endless games of corner tag, especially when boys and girls were allowed in together. Those were the best hours, chasing and diving, splashing and laughing until the lifeguards whistled us out. The pool wasn't just a swimming spot—it was the heartbeat of summer. It was where friendships were made, dares were taken, and every kid in Loma Linda learned what it meant to take the plunge.

Photo credit: Loma Linda Area Parks & Historical Society

By Robert Peterson

In the summer of '67, I left my job at the market and started working as a lifeguard at the local swimming pool. I ended up spending three summers there during college, keeping an eye on swimmers, watching the sun rise and set over the pool deck, and dealing with more than a few strange requests from management.

The head guy, Mac McGurr, was a real character. He had a knack for enforcing pool rules that bordered on the ridiculous. One of his pet policies was a ban on two-piece bathing suits for girls. So here I was, barely 17 or 18, when a girl would stroll in wearing a nice two-piece, and he'd come over with a frown, "Bob, go tell her she can't wear that here." I'd roll my eyes and wonder why he thought I'd be the one to deliver this news. Of all the jobs, this one was probably the worst. Not that I was really complaining...

My time at the pool also gave me a front-row seat to a bit of town history. That summer, Gentry Gym was going up right next to the pool. I'd sit there in the lifeguard chair, watching the construction day by day, the structure slowly taking shape. It was something to witness—brick by brick, beam by beam—as a new part of the community came to life just across the way.

Chapter 32

Gene White

The house didn't look like much from the outside. A small mobile home tucked into a quiet corner of Loma Linda, surrounded by others just like it, neat and unassuming. But if you stepped inside, even just a few feet, you'd know immediately you were in a different world—a world shaped by the imagination of a man who didn't just see things as they were but as they could be.

That was Gene White's way.

Gene lived most of his life in the Inland Empire. Not just *in* it, but *of* it. The dust, the palms, the low golden hills—they were in his blood. He wasn't just a resident; he was a contributor. A doer. A dreamer with dirt on his boots and foam under his fingernails. When most people saw plywood, he saw a mine shaft. When others saw a bare patch of land, he saw ancient ruins or a western frontier. He made fantasies feel local—reachable. You didn't have to go to Disneyland to escape the ordinary. You just had to go where Gene had been.

Before his name meant anything in the world of amusement parks and museum sets, Gene learned the basics the way people used to—hands-on, side by side with his father. They worked houses in Loma Linda, fixing, renting, improving. It wasn't glamorous, but it was real work, and it taught him what mattered. Get it right. Don't cut corners. Be proud of what you leave behind. His father rented homes to university students—often just scraping by—and Gene saw early on how a little stability, a little beauty, could make people feel like they belonged. That feeling stuck with him.

By the time Gene got involved with Knott's Berry Farm, he wasn't there to build roller coasters. He was there to build *worlds*. The Calico Mine Ride was one of the first. If you ever rode it, you probably remember the way it smelled—damp and earthy, like a real mine. That wasn't an accident. Gene made sure every rock face, every lantern, every creak of wood felt believable. He didn't just decorate sets—he lived in the details. And the people who rode that ride, especially the kids, felt like they were part of something big, something dusty and dangerous and exciting. That's what Gene did—he invited people into adventure.

Then came the Log Ride. It wasn't just a flume through fake trees. It was a handcrafted journey through a world he helped create. From the carved wood to the animatronic lumberjacks, every inch bore Gene's fingerprint. Bud Hurlbut might've dreamed the big picture, but Gene brought it into focus. And long after people forgot the names of the creators, they remembered how it *felt*. The splash. The scent of pine. The gasp as the log tipped forward and dropped. That was Gene's art—subtle but unforgettable.

And his reach didn't end at Knott's.

At the Movieland Wax Museum in Buena Park, Gene made movie magic still. He didn't just pose wax figures in scenes—he *built* the scenes. Elaborate, carefully staged, and often surprisingly accurate, they felt like dioramas sprung to life. He took particular pride in the chariot scene from *Ben-Hur*. He'd show off the wheels with their hand-carved knives and point out how the sand looked *just right*. It wasn't enough to copy the movie—it had to *feel* like the movie. Visitors didn't just see Charlton Heston in wax—they *stood in the film*. That was the goal.

The Long Beach Pike was another chapter—one many forget but shouldn't. The Pike wasn't fancy, but it was pure joy, gritty and colorful and alive. Gene's work added layers to that chaos. Funhouses, murals, creature features—whatever they needed, he delivered. No job was too odd. He had a knack for giving even silly things a sense of place. He respected the audience. That's what made his work stand out.

At home, Gene didn't slow down. He took a mobile home—a narrow 20-by-40-foot box—and turned it into a mountain cabin, right there in the University Mobile Estates. Not just rustic, but believable. Shingled wood outside. Rock details that looked quarried, not glued. Inside, a forest mural spanned the living room wall, three-dimensional and lush with artificial plants placed just so, tricking the eye into believing.

He didn't stop there. The bedroom had a window that wasn't a window—just a view of a painted European cityscape lit from above by a carefully placed skylight. The bathroom had an arched tub entry. The dining room lights were handmade cloth chandeliers. And then there was the spa—Gene's masterpiece. Out the back, he built an oasis: fiberglass spa disguised as a natural pond, surrounded by sculpted rocks, toadstools, waterfalls, and actual tree trunks bearing fake leaves. People would walk in and forget they were in a mobile home park. That was the Gene effect.

But not every story is tidy.

In the early 1970s, Gene took a job that looked like fun—designing a sea cave set for *Sigmund and the Sea Monsters*, a children's show produced by Sid and Marty Krofft. Gene, excited as ever, worked with foam materials recommended by MGM, which had assured him they were fire-resistant. They'd even lit samples with matches in front of him—no flame, just char.

Gene built a stunning set—an underwater world above ground, textured and magical. It was a hit. Until a stage light, left too close to the foam, ignited a fire that tore through not just *Sigmund's* set but others nearby—*Barnaby Jones*, *Wild Wild West*. Gone in minutes.

What followed was a mess of finger-pointing. MGM's lawyers filed a $5 million lawsuit, naming the Kroffts, the foam manufacturer, and Gene himself. The weight of it was enormous. He hadn't acted recklessly. He followed instructions, trusted professionals. But that didn't stop the accusations.

Gene fought back. He stood his ground, endured years of legal back-and-forth. Finally, the California Court of Appeals sided with him. MGM was held mostly responsible. The Kroffts bore some of the burden. Gene? Cleared. Vindicated. It didn't erase the stress, but it proved something he already knew—he did things the right way.

And still, he kept creating.

He designed the interior of Kathi's Wigs at Central City Mall. Yes, a wig store. But Gene didn't care what the sign said. He saw a blank slate. He built a foam cave inside the store. Twisting walls. Grotto ceilings. It looked more like an attraction than a salon. And customers—men and women—lined up to see it. His imagination had that kind of pull.

In time, Gene took on one of his biggest thematic challenges: Pharaoh's Kingdom in Redlands. The concept was ambitious—ancient Egypt, but as an immersive theme park. Gene worked alongside his wife, Karen, and daughter, Marlou, to bring it to life. A 40-foot sphinx anchored the entrance. Four towering pharaohs—35 feet each—stood like sentinels. The park's main building was covered in 9,000 sculpted stone tablets. He gave the project his all. Every line in the stone. Every curve in the statues. He didn't believe in shortcuts.

Gene's work was never about ego. He didn't expect awards or fame. What he cared about was whether people *believed* in what he built. Whether a family riding a log through fake wilderness forgot they were in Buena Park for five minutes. Whether a kid standing in front of Cleopatra felt transported. Whether a visitor walking into his spa felt peace.

On August 17, 2014, Gene White passed away at 82. It was the kind of passing that's both quiet and immense. The kind that sneaks up on you weeks later when you visit an old amusement park and realize that rock wall was his. Or you see a chariot in wax and think, "That looks *real*." It is. That's Gene.

He didn't just leave behind rides or sets or murals. He left behind experiences. Memories. A kind of handoff between imagination and reality. And for those of us lucky enough to know him—or even just know his work—he left something else, too: a sense that the world could be made better with a little creativity and a lot of heart.

Gene White didn't just decorate Southern California.

He helped build the stories we tell ourselves when we remember the fun.

Chapter 33

Lupe's Azteca Inn

As I sit here reminiscing, I am filled with fond memories of Lupe's Azteca Inn, a place that holds a special spot in my heart. Located on Hwy 99 (now Redlands Blvd.) and Mountain View in Loma Linda, this unassuming building was home to some of the most incredible Mexican food I've ever had the pleasure of enjoying.

My connection to Lupe's began when I was a young teenager, working summers for an electrical contractor named Ed Buschbacher. My foreman, Arturo Sanchez, would often take us to Lupe's for lunch. Art had a long-standing relationship with the owners of Lupe's, and he would frequently do side work for them. He'd always say, "I'm not eating garbage," when we'd suggest fast food, and instead, he'd take us to Lupe's.

The owner, Lupe, was a kind and warm lady who always made us feel welcome. Her recipes were incredible, and every meal was a treat.

Lupe's originally opened as Lupe's Azteca Inn, but later changed its name to Lupe's Mexican Restaurant. Despite the name change, the food and atmosphere remained the same - warm, welcoming, and full of flavor.

After Lupe passed away, her sister Alta took over the restaurant, and her husband Lencho became a familiar face.

Lencho was a remarkable man who seemed to have a gift for multitasking. He'd sit at the counter, watching TV, reading a book, selling candy, greeting guests, and checking them out all at the same time. It was a feat that never ceased to amaze me. One of Lencho's quirks that still makes me smile was his habit of trying to persuade us to buy a Kit Kat bar on our way out. Whenever we'd give in and buy one, he'd say with a grin, "Here, kitty, kitty, kitty!" It was a small thing, but it's a memory that still brings a smile to my face.

Lupe's was more than just a restaurant; it was an institution. It had been around since the early 1950s, and over the years, it had become a staple in the community. I recall hearing that Lupe's and Lucy's in San Bernardino, as well as Casa De Vikki in Mentone, were all owned by the same family. It was a testament to the family's dedication to serving authentic, delicious Mexican food.

I also remember that before Lupe's expanded into the larger building it occupied for most of its existence, it was a small, narrow building that served beer and sandwiches. There was a sign on the door that read "21" to indicate that it was a bar. Parking was limited, with only a few spots in front of the building and a small lot on the west side.

As I grew older, my appreciation for Lupe's only deepened. I'd often go back to visit, and it was always like stepping into a warm hug. The food was consistently amazing, and the atmosphere was always lively and welcoming. I'd often see familiar faces, including Lencho, who would still be sitting at the counter, watching TV, reading a book, and greeting guests all at the same time.

Lupe's Azteca Inn was a place where time stood still. It was a place where traditions were upheld, and where the love of family and food was always palpable. Even though it's been many years since I last set foot in Lupe's, the memories I made there remain vivid and dear to my heart.

One of the things that made Lupe's so special was the sense of community that permeated every aspect of the restaurant. It was a place where locals gathered to catch up on the latest news and gossip, where families celebrated special occasions, and where friends met to share a meal and some laughter.

Unfortunately, all good things must come to an end. Lupe's Mexican Restaurant eventually closed its doors in the early 2000s. It was a sad day, but the memories I made there will stay with me forever.

For those who were lucky enough to experience Lupe's, you know exactly what I'm talking about. For those who missed out, I'm sorry to say that you'll never know the joy of dining at this incredible establishment. But I hope that by sharing my story, I've been able to give you a glimpse into the magic that was Lupe's Azteca Inn.

Chapter 34
Wallace Koehl

The last time I was in Loma Linda was in 2021, when I spent eight weeks undergoing proton treatment for prostate cancer. It turned out to be a huge success. Driving past the In-N-Out Burger on Tippecanoe during that time stirred an old memory. It wasn't about hamburgers at all. It was about a man named Wallace Koehl, one of my grandfather's old buddies, who always seemed to have his poodle with him—even back in the 1950s.

Wallace owned a little two-bay garage next to his home on Tippecanoe, right about where the In-N-Out stands today. He had a run of bad luck in the late '50s that, strangely enough, ended up turning into good fortune. One Friday afternoon the Loma Linda fire whistle blew, the one we kids could hear all over town, and like always we wondered what was burning down this time. As it turned out, it was Wallace's garage.

It was the middle of summer and he had rigged up a homemade fan on a stand to keep the air moving while he worked. That day he left to pick up some parts. His overhead door used a spring and tension arm assembly, and when he closed it the door jammed into the fan, which was still running. The motor overheated, and before long the place was ablaze. By the time my grandfather and I arrived, the fire crews had just about doused the pile of rubble that had been his shop, his tools, and the two cars he was repairing.

Oddly enough, just a few months earlier Caltrans had informed him that his house and garage sat directly in the path of the new Interstate 10 freeway. He had already signed a contract to sell the property, but at the time of the fire he still owned it—and he was fully insured. Two disasters, the fire and the looming freeway, ended up working in his favor. He collected every bit of insurance money and still received the full pre-fire price from Caltrans.

With that windfall, Wallace moved to 14th Street in Yucaipa, where he bought a two-acre peach grove. Behind the house he built himself a six-bay garage—three times bigger than the old one—and stocked it with all new tools. He went right back to working on cars and trucks and kept at it until he passed away in the late 1980s.

Wallace had a reputation for being a little gruff on the outside, but everyone who knew him also knew he had a heart of gold. He worked on cars for people who depended on them to get to work but couldn't always pay on time. He let them make payments when they could, and he helped more people than most folks ever realized. I was one of them. In my early business days, when I ran into trouble with my truck, he opened a bay of his shop for me, loaned me his tools, and stood by with advice while I overhauled an engine. That experience sealed it for me. I knew right then I would rather be an electrician than a mechanic.

He had his softer side too. When he and his wife moved to Yucaipa, they developed a Sunday ritual that never wavered. Every week, like clockwork, they went up to Law's Coffee Shop and ordered a piece of apple pie. It was their little tradition, steady as the tick of a clock, and it said a lot about who Wallace really was—a man of simple pleasures, loyal habits, and quiet generosity.

And so, passing that In-N-Out in 2021 after my treatment brought it all back—the sound of the old Loma Linda fire whistle, the sight of Wallace with his poodle, the smoking remains of a burned garage, and the way his life turned from loss into abundance. Most of all, it reminded me of his character: tough on the outside, but kind through and through, with nothing but good memories left behind.

Chapter 35
Clarence Harlow

Clarence E. Harlow came to Loma Linda as a boy in 1908, when the town was little more than a scattering of pepper trees and a new medical school trying to find its footing. His father, Alfred, had moved the family from Walla Walla, Washington, after hearing that the Seventh-day

Adventist Church was building a sanitarium and a school for doctors in Southern California. Alfred was among the first medical students enrolled in the program. The stories of those days were passed down to Clarence: how there was only one automobile in the entire town, how the students had to walk the Southern Pacific tracks to Colton for their laboratory work, and how the school survived more on faith than on resources. That persistence and faith left its mark on Clarence, who grew up to embody the same steady resolve in business and in civic life.

Clarence attended the church on the hill, the first Adventist congregation in the town, before the Campus Hill Church was built. He studied at Loma Linda Academy and later took pre-med courses at La Sierra University in Riverside, but his future lay not in medicine, as it had for his father, but in the more practical work of meeting the daily needs of his neighbors. In the 1920s he bought the Loma Linda Ice Company and for fifteen years delivered blocks of ice door to door. At first by wagon, and later by truck, he sweated through long summer days hauling the frozen blocks that kept families' iceboxes cool. By doing so he came to know almost every household in town. He used to say he outsold every salesman because he had already sold everyone ice.

In 1933 Clarence married Emily, and together they built a marriage that would last for more than seventy years. Two years later, in 1935, he opened his first appliance store in the old Loma Linda Bank building. Business was steady, and in the early 1940s he moved into the space vacated by the Emerson Market, a location that put him right in the center of town. His knack for timing and adaptation never failed him. As gas refrigeration became available, he began selling Servel refrigerators, eventually adding Maytag washers, Frigidaire refrigerators, and every other appliance needed by the growing community. What had begun with ice delivery expanded into a thriving store that served families for decades.

His success was recognized beyond Loma Linda. In 1954 Clarence was one of six appliance dealers in Southern California to win the grand prize in the Servel Gas Refrigerator sales contest. The prize was a trip to New York, where Clarence and Emily stayed at the Waldorf-Astoria Hotel and sat in box seats at the World Series between the Cleveland Indians and the New York Giants. For a couple who had built their life in a small California town, the trip was both reward and affirmation. Clarence had come a long way from hauling blocks of ice through dusty streets.

The town changed as well, and so did his business. By the early 1960s Loma Linda University planned expansion for its new dental school, and the building where Harlow's store stood was scheduled for demolition. Clarence did not resist progress. In 1964 he moved into a new building at 10267 Tippecanoe Street, just north of Highway 99. The new store was modern for its time, built of stucco and frame, air-conditioned, brightly lit, with a large showroom beside a warehouse and service shop. Customers could browse more than sixty thousand dollars' worth of appliances in one location. For the grand opening, which lasted four days, Clarence and Emily welcomed friends and neighbors with refreshments, prizes, and the sense of optimism that marked Loma Linda's growth in that decade. The new location carried the Harlow name forward, even as the old store made way for the university's future.

Clarence never ran for political office, but he became one of the town's most consistent civic voices. In the late 1940s he joined with neighbors to demand sidewalks and traffic lights from the county. When the county hesitated, the group pressed harder and won. That success led to the founding of the Chamber of Commerce in 1959. A few years later, the same group pushed for incorporation, and Clarence argued plainly that unless Loma Linda became its own city, San Bernardino would absorb it. That argument settled the issue, and Loma Linda became a city in its own right. Clarence continued to attend council meetings, offering his opinions on issues like flood control and finances. Friends like Councilman Elmer Digneo described him as always interested, always active, and always contributing, even if he avoided the spotlight.

From the house where he lived for more than thirty years, Clarence kept watch on the city he had helped shape. Emily remarked that he always found a way to be in the middle of things, though he never cared for taking credit. He built a reputation not just as a businessman but as a steady hand in the community. By the mid-1990s he was ninety-five years old, still sharp, still attending meetings when he could, and still reflecting on the long arc of his life in the town. He put it simply: he was the history of the town. No one else alive had lived in Loma Linda as long as he had.

Clarence's legacy was inseparable from his father's. Alfred had been one of the school's pioneer medical students, walking the railroad tracks to Colton for classes. Clarence carried that same determination into his own work, shaping the community through business, persistence, and civic leadership. From the days when he delivered ice in the 1920s, through the opening of his first appliance store in 1935, to the grand opening of his modern Tippecanoe Street showroom in 1964, Clarence's life mirrored the growth of Loma Linda itself. He and Emily built a family, raised their son Claude, and together turned a modest delivery route into a business known across the Inland Empire. The Harlow name endured on storefronts, in civic groups, and in the memories of the people he served. When asked to sum up his place in the community, Clarence needed only one line. I'm the history of the town, he said, and in truth, he was.

Chapter 36

Here Is the Church, Here Is the Steeple...

Credit: Loma Linda University Digital Archives

In the early 1950s, the conversation that had been quietly simmering in the corners of Burden Hall suddenly came to the surface. The College Church had long gathered in that building, a modest structure dedicated back in 1934. At the time, it had been more than adequate, a practical auditorium that doubled as a sanctuary, but Loma Linda was no longer the small outpost it had been in the Depression years. The medical school had grown, the hospital on the hill was humming with patients and staff, and the membership rolls swelled with faculty, students, and families who needed something bigger, more permanent, and more dignified than Burden Hall. The conclusion was clear: the College Church would need to be replaced.

What began in whispers turned into formal planning sessions, committees, and eventually, in the mid-1950s, an organized push to build a proper University Church. The idea was not just to replace Burden Hall, but to make a statement—this was now the spiritual center of a university, and it demanded a structure to match.

Yet in the midst of that planning, there was a curious cultural quirk in town. To outsiders, the Adventist community in Loma Linda may have looked unified, but if you lived there you knew that there were really two "tribes." There were the Burden Hall Adventists and the Hill Church Adventists. The Hill Church sat right beside the hospital on the hill, an unmistakable landmark both for worshippers and for patients looking out the hospital windows. It was larger, the dominant congregation in town, while Burden Hall always felt more like a small auditorium that did its best to keep up.

The distinction between the two groups was never very clear, at least not to a boy trying to make sense of it. Families you thought might be Hill Church folks sometimes turned up at Burden, and vice versa. From the outside it almost felt arbitrary. Yet there was no denying the size difference: the Hill Church was the big player, and Burden Hall always carried the sense of being smaller, provisional, almost temporary.

That dynamic began to shift when the University Church project got underway. The very act of tearing down an orange grove to make room for a new sanctuary signaled something. Allegiances that had once been split between Hill and Burden began to coalesce. Here was a building that would be worthy of the community's aspirations, one that looked like it belonged to a university medical center. The gravitational pull was too strong to resist.

My own first memory of the University Church is tied to that orange grove. I remember when the trees came down and the very first thing to rise was the steeple. What made it unusual was how they built it. Instead of pouring the entire tower in one monumental effort, they used a slip form system. They started on the ground and then inched their way skyward in small increments—eight inches at a time. The process fascinated me.

The idea was simple but ingenious: as the concrete set, the formwork was slowly jacked upward, so the weight of the new concrete was borne by the structure itself. The critical trick was avoiding cold joints. If the concrete set too long before the next batch was added, you would get a visible seam, a weakness in the tower. To prevent that, the workers had to keep the pour going around the clock.

I can still see it in my mind: the glow of lights on the top of the tower late at night, the hum of activity, and the cement trucks arriving long past bedtime. I distinctly remember one night around eleven o'clock, seeing a mixer churning away and men at work. The steeple had become a twenty-four-hour operation. It took nearly two weeks of constant pouring to finish, the tower slowly climbing into the sky like a concrete plant reaching maturity.

It was a remarkable sight for a community used to orange groves and small wooden chapels. Here, in the middle of the lot, a slender white steeple pushed higher each day, the first unmistakable sign that the University Church was real. Everything else—walls, sanctuary, classrooms—would follow later. But the steeple stood as the herald of what was to come.

Of course, in a community bound by Sabbath traditions, there were questions. I don't recall exactly how they handled the sundown Friday to sundown Saturday window, but I do remember the work never seemed to stop. If there were accommodations, they were invisible to me. From my vantage point as a boy, the tower rose day after day without pause, a living thing fed by concrete and steel, overseen by men who looked impossibly busy.

That steeple became a landmark, not just for Loma Linda but for my own memories. To this day, when I picture the University Church, I first picture the steeple—not the sanctuary or the pews, but that slender tower born in eight-inch increments of determination.

Once the building was complete, the story shifted from construction to upkeep, and with it came the fundraisers. It seemed as though no sooner had we settled into the pews than the congregation was reminded of the next great need. First came the remodel campaign. Later came the push for a proper pipe organ. And then there were other drives—each with its own air of excitement, cajoling, and the ever-present thermometer.

My strongest memory of those efforts is tied to Milton Murray. If Burden Hall had been the center of worship, Milton was the center of fundraising. He had a way of standing up each Sabbath and making money sound almost sacramental. With his commanding presence and endless optimism, he turned what might have been dry appeals into moments of drama.

Every week the thermometer stood waiting. It was a large, bold display, with a towering frame and a bright red column that slowly crept upward. Milton would march up to it, marker in hand, and with exaggerated ceremony fill in just a bit more of that red line. The congregation leaned forward, whispering about whether they would hit the next milestone. It was theater as much as accounting, and Milton knew it.

There was also a smaller version of the thermometer placed outside by the road. It was less impressive, a little weather-worn, but it mattered in its own way. People driving by could see the progress, measure the community's determination, and feel a nudge of pride. Week after week, that red column climbed higher, signaling that the University Church was not just surviving but thriving.

Looking back, the irony is almost humorous: the remodel and organ fundraisers ended up costing more than it had taken to build the church in the first place. Yet that was beside the point. The value lay in the spirit, in the way the community rallied together, and in how Milton's thermometer became a shared symbol of what could be accomplished when everyone pulled in the same direction.

The University Church, as it finally stood, was a monument not just to architecture but to the culture of a place and time. It replaced Burden Hall, bridged the gap between the Burden Hall Adventists and the Hill Church Adventists, and gave the university a spiritual home that felt equal to its mission. For me, it also carried the unforgettable memories of a steeple built in the glow of floodlights, concrete poured through the night, and a red thermometer slowly climbing its way toward a future no one could have quite imagined back in the modest days of 1934.

University Church

As a young boy, he vividly remembered the university church's ambitious fundraising efforts. Every Sabbath, Milton Murray—known across the community as the ultimate church fundraiser—would take center stage, commanding the congregation's attention. Milton's dedication to raising funds for the church was practically legendary, and his updates became a weekly ritual that defined the drive to remodel the beloved building.

Each week, Milton would reveal his famous fundraising thermometer, a towering display with bold lines and a slowly rising red column, prominently placed at the front of the sanctuary. With an air of excitement, he would update everyone on the progress, pointing out how close they were to reaching the grand goal of $150,000—a staggering amount at the time. The hope was that if they reached a certain amount in seed money, the conference would match it, allowing construction to begin.

Milton made a show of filling in the thermometer each week, meticulously shading in small red increments as they edged closer to the target. The congregation watched eagerly, whispering among themselves, wondering if this might be the week they'd hit another milestone. The thermometer became more than just a fundraising tool; it was a shared symbol of hope, commitment, and unity.

Outside by the road, a smaller version of the thermometer was set up, weathering the elements but standing as a constant reminder of the church's mission. It was visible to anyone passing by, showing off the progress and pride of the community.

Looking back, the irony was clear: the cost of remodeling the University Church far exceeded what it had taken to build the original structure. But the value wasn't just in the money raised; it was in the spirit of community, the shared goal, and the sense of excitement that Milton and his thermometer brought to everyone each week.

Chapter 37
Campus Snack Shop

Credit: Loma Linda University Digital Archives

This picture brings back a flood of memories for me, each detail sparking another. First, I remember the boxy little signs with bold letters that lined the downtown center, with their stark black-and-white contrast that seemed to command attention. And then there were the strange shaped fluorescent lights, whose peculiar shape intrigued me. I once pointed out to someone upstairs in the Trust Department that these lights were shaped like the clubs symbol in a deck of cards. For some reason, this observation unsettled them, as if I had somehow revealed a flaw in their design. But those lights and signs aren't the focus here. What really caught my eye, and what this story is truly about, is the Campus Snack Shop.

If you look to the right side of this picture, you'll see the snack shop, modestly tucked into the building with its small, curtained windows. This was a place filled with charm, a cozy little corner that held its own among the bustling cafeteria setting. For those who worked and lived in the area, the Campus Snack Shop was more than just a snack bar—it was a small escape where you could sit down, relax, and enjoy a moment's peace. The curtained windows gave it a homely feel, making it a beloved spot for many.

This particular photo is the only one I could find with any kind of decent resolution that captures the Campus Snack Shop. Although the resolution isn't perfect, for the purposes of preserving this memory, it will do.

At that time, I lived in Mentone and was neighbors with one of the General Telephone supervisors in Redlands named Bill Kingsley. He had a tradition for welcoming new hires to the area. Whenever a new to the Inland Empire employee joined their ranks, he'd send them on a job assignment to Loma Linda and suggest they visit the Campus Snack Shop. For fresh recruits, this recommendation usually led to a baffling yet memorable experience. The following exchange is a classic example of what typically ensued. I will call the telephone man Bob.

Waitress: Welcome to the Campus Snack Shop.

Bob: Hi! I've heard this place has really good food. Can I have a cup of coffee while I look at the menu?

Waitress: I'm sorry, sir, but we don't serve coffee. We do offer Postum, however.

Bob: Postum? Uhh, that's okay—just give me a Coke.

Waitress: I'm sorry, sir, we don't have Coke. I can bring you a glass of orange soda, 7 Up, lemonade.

Bob: Lemonade? OK, but let me take a look at the menu first. Actually, all I really want is a cheeseburger.

Waitress: I'm sorry, sir. We don't serve cheeseburgers, but we do have veggie burgers.

Bob: Do you have fried chicken?

Waitress: I'm very sorry sir. Would you like a bowl of meatless chili with a whole wheat roll?

Bob: Oh goof grief, never mind, I'll just go somewhere else. Where's the cigarette machine?

Although every story Bill heard was different, the end result, however. almost was almost exactly the same.

Chapter 38

How La Sierra College almost ended up in Yucaipa

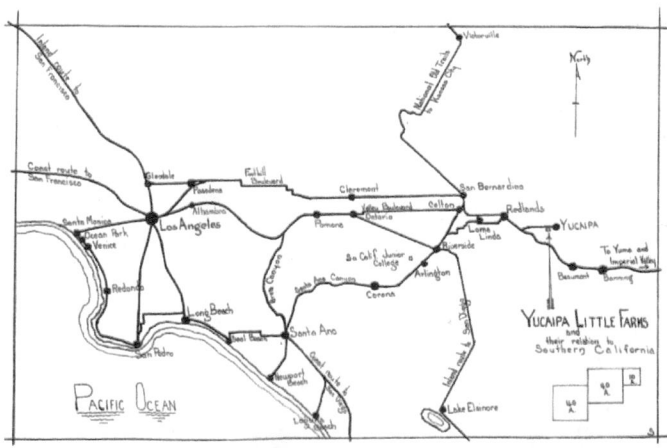

Yucaipa Little Farms map
Credit: Loma Linda University Digital Archives

Yucaipa University almost happened 100 years ago. This is a story of how a businessman, a doctor, and a minister changed the path of 2 communities in the Inland Empire

Former Redlands resident Richard F. (Dick) Emmerson once said of himself, "I've never done anything I've lost money on." Emmerson was a kind of efficiency expert, and his employer would often send him to places that were losing money.

Emmerson had just proved himself once again as assistant manager and purchasing agent for the White Memorial Hospital in Los Angeles when his employers asked him to sit on a committee with Dr. Henry Vollmer and Pastor Burden of Loma Linda. The committee's task was to select a site for a new boarding high school in Southern California.

The committee almost selected Dunlap Acres that was referred to as "Yucaipa Little Farms" in Yucaipa. It belonged to farmers, but the 3 decided that it was too close to Loma Linda and chose to buy property in La Sierra instead.

Emmerson, being the businessman on the committee, made connection with W.J. Hole, who owned a 17,000-acre ranch, Rancho La Sierra, between Riverside and Corona. (Side note, La Sierra was not his only ranch. He also owned Rancho La Habra -now known as just plain La Habra)

Emmerson negotiated the purchase of 400 acres for the new school. He also purchased 25 acres for himself.

"He bought the additional acreage for $485 an acre. His wife once asked, 'Why did you buy so much land? Why not just enough for a house?'" Emmerson always answered, "The school needs that property and I'm going to sell it to the school." True to his word, Emmerson sold the land to the school for the same price he paid for it, despite offers from Safeway and another store to buy the land at much higher prices.

In an interesting turn of events, Richard Emmerson went on to start a new business in Redlands—Emmerson Mortuary (now known as Emmerson-Bartlett Memorial Chapel) which later handled the funerals for both Dr. Vollmer and Pastor Burden.

Chapter 39

The Great Loma Linda Academy Fire of 1947

Photo Credit: Loma Linda Area parks & Historical Society

March of 1947 was supposed to be a fresh start for Loma Linda Academy. With a new campus standing tall on Anderson Avenue, nestled near the sanitarium and the college, it was a beacon of hope and growth for the Loma Linda community. The freshly rebuilt classrooms, administrative offices, and the spacious auditorium were symbols of progress, each space holding the aspirations of a close-knit community. But that promise went up in flames on a quiet, unsuspecting night.

The fire broke out just before midnight, shattering the calm of the small town. Most residents had already settled in for the night, and silence blanketed the streets. H.S. Nelson, the sanitarium manager, jolted awake to the sound of a ringing phone. Moments later, he was racing toward the academy, his mind grappling with the news. What he found when he arrived was a sight that no one wanted to see: flames devouring the academy's front wing, especially around the administrative offices. As the fire blazed, Loma Linda residents gathered in shock, helplessly watching the place where their children learned and grew up turn to ash.

Photo Credit: Loma Linda Area parks & Historical Society

The investigation that followed painted a grim picture. Scattered evidence at the scene pointed to arson, a realization that added a heavy weight to the loss. Back then, instead of red flares, people used smudge pots filled with oil that would burn all night, casting a steady glow. It was one of these smudge pots was found thrown the academy's business office window, a makeshift torch left among the charred records and files. The official cause of the fire was ruled as arson, but despite whispers around town, no one was ever arrested or charged. The mystery lingered, adding an air of tragedy and unease to the already devastating loss.

Photo Credit: Loma Linda Area parks & Historical Society

The day after the fire, the community rallied to salvage what they could. A call went out for volunteers to sift through the rubble, hoping to recover any items or materials that might still be useful. Among the first to arrive was my grandfather, a true pack rat who saw potential in the strangest of finds. After a long day of sifting through the debris, he returned home with a truckload of charred but usable lockers. Though many of the lockers were damaged beyond repair, he managed to rescue a few prime pieces, taking them back to his basement. (much to my grandmothers chagrin)

Years passed, and my grandfather's resourcefulness kept those lockers in circulation. When he bought a new International truck in 1952, he saw an opportunity. The lockers were converted storage bins in the back of his truck, giving the old metal pieces a new lease on life. Even when he sold the truck, he carefully removed the lockers and stored them.

When I started my own business, those lockers made their way into my life. I bought an old plumbing van from George Randolph - a old, rugged and dependable workhorse of a vehicle. The lockers fit perfectly, and I used them as storage, organizing my tools and parts just as my grandfather had done. For years, they traveled with me. And even when I eventually sold that van, I couldn't bear to part with them. I pulled them out and moved them to my shop on Gardena Street, where they served as storage for many more years, a quiet witness to that night in 1947.

These lockers became more than just a set of shelves; they were like a family heirloom, passed down, adapted, and preserved. They remained with me until 1994 when I sold the Gardena Street building, and at last, I let them go.

Chapter 40

Moving Day

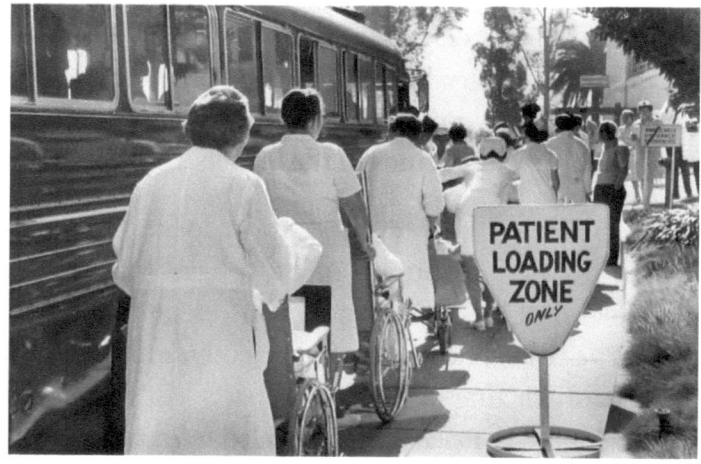

Credit: Loma Linda University Digital Archives

Moving day in Loma Linda came on a blistering Sunday, July 9, 1967. Everybody knew it was coming, but knowing and seeing were two different things. By late morning the thermometer was pressing into the upper nineties, the kind of heat that makes the asphalt shimmer and the air feel like you're looking through rippled glass. The smell of dust and tar hung in the valley, and even the pepper trees along Anderson Street seemed to sag under the weight of the day.

The old hospital on the hill had been our steady neighbor since 1929. Its windows glowed like a lantern at night, a familiar sight above the citrus groves. People were born there, people died there, and everyone in between had walked its hallways. But by the 1960s it was crowded and worn. We had all been watching the new hospital rise since 1964, three circular towers with a central hub, nine stories above ground and two below. Some laughed that it looked like a freeway cloverleaf, and the nickname stuck. Whatever people thought of the design, there was no denying it was the future. Two thousand rooms, they said, though only three hundred and twenty were finished and ready for opening day.

That morning, the Army arrived. You could hear them coming down Barton Road, a low rumble that built until the first trucks rolled into view. Then came more trucks, a bus, ambulances, even passenger cars. Colonel Homer O. Stilson, a West Covina physician, stepped out in uniform, flanked by Army Reserve medical corpsmen of the 349th General Hospital, 15th U.S. Army Corps. They had come from the General Patton Reserve Center in Maywood, pressed and polished, ready to carry out one of the strangest missions of their careers: moving a hospital bed by bed.

Credit: Loma Linda University Digital Archives

The military hadn't come alone. Fort MacArthur had sent vehicles, so had Norton Air Force Base, March Air Force Base, the Naval Station at Terminal Island, and the Marine Air Station at El Toro. To the townsfolk who gathered along Anderson Street, it felt like the whole U.S. military had rolled into Loma Linda for the day. Mothers shaded their children with umbrellas, men loosened their collars, and teenagers pedaled up on bikes to watch. And when the first patients began coming out, the crowd fell quiet.

There were 125 patients to move, reduced from the usual 180 so the job wouldn't overwhelm the staff. Those strong enough to walk climbed onto a military bus, each with a nurse beside them. The weaker ones were carried on stretchers, soldiers steadying each end, then eased into ambulances where they rode two at a time, always with a nurse watching over them. The sickest of all went bed and all, rolled out under the hot sun and into moving vans, the nurses climbing in behind them, and sometimes a doctor too. It was one thing to read about it in the newspaper. It was another to see your neighbor's entire sickroom vanish into the back of a truck and drive down the hill.

Wallace E. Platner, the hospital's administrative assistant, was everywhere at once. Clipboard in hand, sweat darkening his shirt, he directed vehicles, checked off names, and reassured families. He looked like a man trying to keep a parade in step, except this parade couldn't afford to drop a single float.

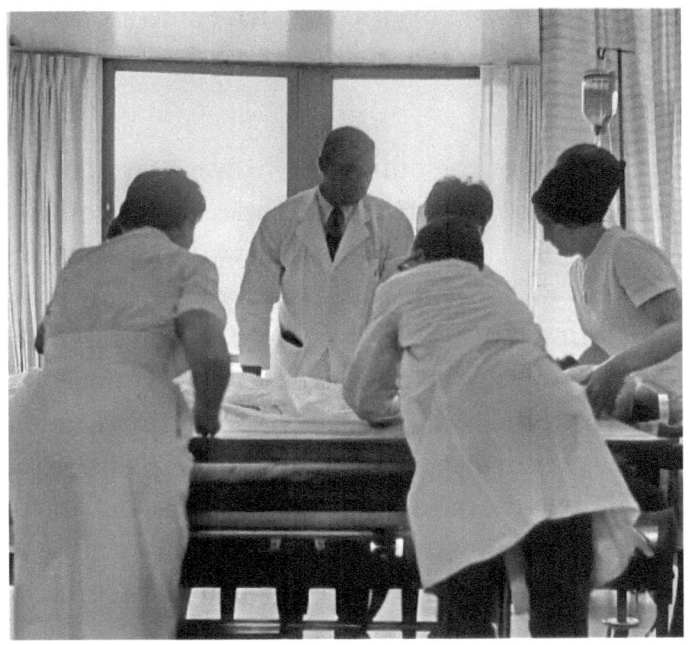

Credit: Loma Linda University Digital Archives

And the town itself had turned out. More volunteers than there were jobs. Church members, students, townsfolk all offering to push wheelchairs, carry charts, run messages. You couldn't walk ten feet without stumbling into someone ready to help. For once the hospital didn't have to ask; the whole town simply showed up, because everyone understood they were watching history.

Down Anderson Street the convoy rolled: buses, ambulances, trucks, each loaded with someone's neighbor, someone's grandmother, someone's child. The heat shimmered off the road, and people muttered, "Hot day to be hauling beds," but no one left. A boy on his bicycle pointed out Mrs. Johnson from church. Another swore he saw the town's postman wave from a stretcher. Someone passed out paper cups of water, and still the crowd stood, unwilling to miss a moment.

At the bottom of the hill the new towers gleamed in the sun, strange and futuristic. Nine stories above ground, two below, eleven levels in all. More than two thousand rooms, though only three hundred and twenty were ready that day. The nurses loved the new design: from the central station in each round tower, they could see every bed at once. It gave them a sense of control and safety, something the old hospital had never managed. Of course, making square rooms out of a circle meant the bathrooms came out in funny little triangles, a quirk people laughed about on the tours before opening. But even with triangular bathrooms, it was a marvel compared to the old wards.

Credit: Loma Linda University Digital Archives

There was more. The towers had been built with 1967's most advanced earthquake protections. Nine inches of shock absorbers separated each wing, allowing the towers to sway independently if a quake hit. Engineers bragged that it was a building that could dance when the earth moved. For a town that knew the San Andreas Fault ran not so far away, it was a comfort.

And then there was the computer. During the tours before the opening, the guides had ushered townspeople into a chilled room full of blinking lights and humming cabinets. It was a computer system, they said, the most advanced any hospital had ever had. But the jaw-dropper was this: Loma Linda's system was linked to UCLA's by a telephone line. For the first time in history, two hospitals could talk to each other by machine. It was something the government had been doing for years, but no hospitals had ever tried it. People whispered that it was like science fiction, the beginning of something that might one day connect the whole world. No one called it the internet yet, but that's what it was, the first faint outline of it, humming away in a basement under the hot July sun.

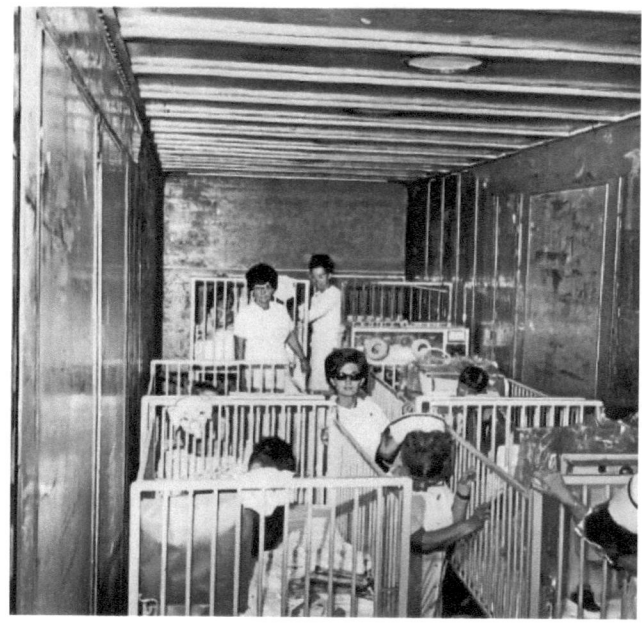

Credit: Loma Linda University Digital Archives

Inside, nurses waited in starched uniforms, smiling as each patient arrived. They moved quickly but gently, checking charts, settling people into fresh rooms. Families followed, anxious and relieved at once. For the patients themselves, the move was often just a blur of sunlight, uniforms, and jolting wheels. But for everyone watching—nurses, doctors, townsfolk—it was unforgettable.

By late afternoon, the last bed had been rolled into place, the last ambulance parked, the last clipboard checked. The towers were alive now, humming with voices and footsteps. Up on the hill, the old hospital sat quiet for the first time in nearly four decades. That night the ridge above town was dark, no glow in the windows, no beacon over the groves. Neighbors stepped onto porches and looked up, expecting the familiar lantern, and saw only stars.

Over supper tables the talk was all about the move. People marveled that it had gone so smoothly. Not a patient lost, not a stumble, not a slip. Someone joked that their own moving day looked like a circus compared to this. Others admitted they'd miss the sight of the old hospital on the hill, but most spoke with pride. Pride that their little town now had towers you could see from miles away, a hospital as modern as anything in Los Angeles, the only full university medical center between here and Houston.

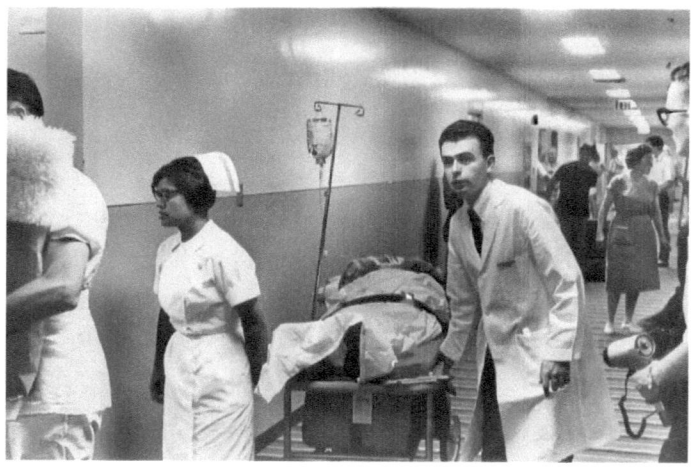

Credit: Loma Linda University Digital Archives

The children told the story with the most excitement. They imitated the growl of the trucks, the squeak of the stretcher wheels, the bark of the colonel's orders. They remembered the soldiers' boots, the nurses' calm voices, the line of vehicles stretching longer than any parade. Some swore they had waved at a patient who waved back. Others bragged that they had touched one of the moving vans and that made them part of history. And years later, those same children told their own children, "I was there the day they moved the hospital."

It was more than a change of address. It was the day the very center of Loma Linda shifted from the hilltop to the valley floor. The cloverleaf towers would go on to see triumphs and tragedies, births and losses, innovations that would make headlines and quiet daily mercies that never would. But July 9, 1967, would always stand apart. It was the day the Army came, the town gathered, the volunteers outnumbered the jobs, and the hospital itself got up and moved. For those of us who stood sweating in the 95-degree heat, watching neighbors roll past in buses and moving vans, it was unforgettable. It wasn't just the patients who moved that day. In its own way, the whole town moved too.

Chapter 41

Hulda

In the 1960s my grandfather did a lot of side jobs, and a surprising number of them seemed to come from little old ladies. One of them was a lady named Hulda. She lived in Loma Linda and she was very nice, always soft-spoken and gracious, but her phone calls to our house followed the exact same pattern every single time.

The call would start with her gentle voice saying, "Hello, is Amos there?" I would answer that he wasn't home, and ask if I could take a message. That's when the script kicked in. First she would carefully explain the electrical problem she was having. Then she would always add that although she did most of her own home repairs and all of her yard work, she was "scared to death of electricity." Next, she would give a glowing compliment about what a wonderful person and great electrician my grandfather was. And finally, she would wander into a little conversation about diet and exercise. That was her exact four-point outline, every single time she called.

To me, she was just a kind woman who needed my grandfather to come by and fix a switch or a socket. I had no idea she was anybody special. In fact, I didn't think much about her at all—until about ten years later, when I stumbled across a documentary about her and realized that Hulda Crooks was something extraordinary. The sweet little lady who was terrified of electricity was better known to the rest of the world as "Grandma Whitney," the woman who became famous for climbing Mount Whitney well into her nineties.

She didn't even start until she was sixty-six years old. That was in 1962, her first ascent of Mount Whitney, which at 14,505 feet is the tallest peak in the continental United States. And after that, she didn't just stop with one climb. She kept doing it, almost every year, until her last climb when she was ninety-one. Think about that. Ninety-one years old, and still strong enough to make the long, lung-burning, foot-pounding trek up the rocky spine of the Sierra Nevada. At that age most people are proud to shuffle a block or two around their neighborhood. Hulda was climbing over 14,000 feet of mountain.

And Whitney wasn't her only conquest. She also became the oldest woman to climb Mount Fuji in Japan, which she did at age ninety-one, the very same year she made her last Whitney climb. She knocked off dozens of other peaks in

California, and over time she completed the 212-mile John Muir Trail, piece by piece. To say she was active is like saying Michael Jordan was pretty good at basketball. She was in a whole different league.

Her feats didn't go unnoticed. Congressman Jerry Lewis from California took up her cause and worked for five years to get one of the jagged peaks next to Whitney renamed in her honor. Congress doesn't like naming things after living people, but eventually he got it through, and in 1990 the old Day Needle officially became Crooks Peak. The next year they flew her up in a helicopter along with the Congressman for a little ceremony to mark the occasion. By then, she had already proven to the world that she could get there under her own power, but it was nice to see her recognized while she was still alive.

The media loved her too. Reporters tagged along with her on the trail, sweating and gasping behind this tiny grandmother who just kept moving uphill like a machine. There's a video of her twentieth Whitney climb that I edited down to less than ten minutes. She had three reporters with her, all of them puffing and panting, while Hulda just kept her steady pace with a floppy sunhat shading her face. They'd try to interview her between switchbacks, and she'd give them her thoughts on diet, health, and life while still pushing upward without missing a beat. Watching that video was the closest I was ever going to get to the top of Whitney myself.

What struck me most wasn't just what she did, but how she did it. She wasn't trying to break records or show anybody up. She simply believed that health and exercise and a positive outlook were worth practicing every single day. She was a vegetarian her whole life, long before it was trendy. She walked every day. She kept herself active, not in a frantic or punishing way, but in the steady, methodical way she climbed mountains. She'd say that eating right and staying active were essential, and then she would go out and prove it by lacing up her boots.

She even dabbled in track. In 1982, when most people her age were picking out retirement homes, she entered the Senior Olympics and set a world record for the fastest woman to run 1500 meters. She wasn't satisfied with being a mountain goat; she was also fleet of foot on a track. At age ninety-five she was still walking two miles a day. She finally passed away in 1997 at the age of 101, a full century of life lived with purpose, long after most of her peers were gone.

She had started life far from Loma Linda, born in 1896 in Saskatchewan, Canada. As a girl she was frail and sickly, plagued by tuberculosis and an overfondness for candy and meat. It wasn't until her teenage years, after moving to California and embracing the Seventh-day Adventist tradition of vegetarianism, that she began to see what health really meant. She studied dietetics at Loma Linda University, graduating in 1927, and later worked as a dietitian and researcher. She co-wrote scientific papers about vegetarian nutrition decades before the rest of the world started catching up. She married Dr. Samuel Crooks, who became a physician in Loma Linda, but he died in 1950. Widowed at midlife, she turned to hiking as both solace and renewal. What began as grief therapy became her life's defining adventure.

Even presidents took note of her. Ronald Reagan and George H. W. Bush both sent her letters praising her achievements, calling her an inspiration and a reminder that America still valued vitality and courage at any age. Imagine that—one of my grandfather's customers, the same woman who used to call our house timidly asking for help with her wiring, was getting letters from the White House.

Back home in Loma Linda, the city honored her by naming Hulda Crooks Park after her. It sits at the base of the South Hills, with trails, courts, and playgrounds where kids run and joggers loop around without even knowing whose name is on the sign. There's a bronze likeness of her there, gazing out over the hills, a reminder that the woman who could barely work up the nerve to touch a light switch could, in fact, walk clear across the Sierra Nevada.

What I've always loved about her story is the contrast. To me, as a kid, she was the timid little lady on the phone who was scared stiff of electricity. She'd call, describe her wiring problem, heap compliments on my grandfather, then give her speech about diet and exercise. She never hinted that she was doing anything more adventurous than pulling weeds or tinkering in her yard. Yet, away from the telephone, she was out climbing mountains, setting records, and doing things that left younger, stronger people trailing in her dust.

It's humbling to think about. I couldn't do half of what she did when I was half her age. The only small consolation I have is that, unlike Hulda, I was never afraid of electricity. But then again, maybe being scared of one thing gave her the courage to conquer everything else.

Hulda never thought of herself as special. She described herself as a late bloomer, someone who took up hiking because she needed healing after her husband's death. She had been a sickly child and a widow for nearly fifty years. She was supposed to be slowing down. Instead, she was finding a whole new life on the trail. That's why her story touched so many people. She showed the world that it's never too late to find adventure, never too late to take that first step up the mountain.

When she died at 101, the obituaries didn't have to work very hard. They wrote themselves: the oldest woman to climb Mount Whitney, the oldest woman to climb Mount Fuji, the Senior Olympic record holder, the hiker who proved that age is not a wall but a horizon.

And for me, I'll always remember her both ways—the lady who was scared to death of electrical wiring, and the same lady who stood proudly on top of the highest peak in California, looking out over the whole state.

If you'd like to see what it was really like to climb Whitney with her, I've linked the edited video of her twentieth ascent with reporters trailing behind her. You'll find the QR code at the end of this story.

Chapter 42
Herluf Jensen

Credit: Lomasphere

When I look back on my school years, I can say with certainty that principals and I were not strangers. From first and second grade at Loma Linda, through my long stretch at Redlands Junior Academy from third to tenth, and finally back to Loma Linda Academy for my junior and senior years, it wasn't unusual to hear that the principal wanted to see me. Usually it meant trouble of some sort. That's why it felt so odd when I learned that the former principal of Loma Linda Academy, a man I had never even met, wanted to talk with me. His name was Herluf L. Jensen.

By the time I was enrolled at Loma Linda Academy, Jensen had already moved on. He had been principal there for just one year, tucked in between the tenures of Elmer Digneo and A. Herbert Johns. So my first thought was, what could this man possibly want with me? And my second thought was, whatever it was, it couldn't be good.

Still, curiosity won out, and we arranged to meet. The place he chose was the parking lot next to the old campus cafeteria. Not an office, not a boardroom — just the cafeteria lot where students and teachers had crossed paths for years. I walked up expecting a stern conversation with a man I didn't know. What I found instead was a kind smile and a handshake.

From the moment we met, it was clear he wasn't looking to discipline me. He had that rare quality of making you feel comfortable right away. He explained that though he had been principal at the Academy, he was now working for the University Trust Department, temporarily heading up the Real Estate Division. That department managed just about everything the University Foundation owned, with the exception of the hospital and the school itself. The list was long: commercial buildings in town, dozens of rental houses scattered around Loma Linda and beyond, and even properties in other states. They had a maintenance man, but no electrician.

Then he got to the point. He told me he had heard through the grapevine that I already had my own electrical business. I was only a junior in high school, working under my grandfather's contractor's license, trying to build up enough work to keep busy. It didn't feel like much to me. But to Jensen, it was impressive. He said he liked to help young people any way he could, and then he asked if I'd be interested in doing work for the University's properties.

That simple offer probably changed the course of my life more than anything else in those years.

I didn't hesitate. Steady work wasn't easy to come by, and the chance to work for an institution like the University was golden. Soon enough, I was answering calls for them, and no two days were the same. One day I'd be sweating it out in the attic of the old Loma Linda Market, pulling wire through rafters and wiping dust from my eyes. The next day I'd be crawling under a rental house with a flashlight in my teeth, pushing through cobwebs and dirt to chase down an electrical fault. The work was varied, sometimes tough, but it was real work, and I was grateful for every bit of it.

A year later, when the University brought in Dick Parks as the permanent Real Estate manager, I was already well established. By then I'd done enough jobs for them that I was part of their routine. And from there, the relationship only grew stronger. The University turned out to be the single best customer I had during my first ten years in business. They gave me steady calls, consistent work, and more importantly, the kind of reputation that helped me get established. Looking back, I don't think I could have built my business in quite the same way without that early boost.

The funny thing is, it all started with a man who wasn't even my principal, a man I had never once met before he asked me to come to that cafeteria parking lot. He had no reason to reach out to me, no obligation. But he did, and his kindness gave me the break I needed. Sadly, I never had the chance to tell Mr. Jensen how much that moment meant to me. He passed away in 2003, just a month after his wife, Bernadette. But I've never forgotten him, and I couldn't write about Loma Linda without paying tribute to the man who gave me the start of my career.

As for Mr. Jensen himself, his story was remarkable in its own right. He was born on December 31, 1921, in Minnesota, to Danish-American parents who valued education and hard work. Like so many of his generation, his early adult years were shaped by the war. Drafted into the U.S. Army, he spent three years overseas as a medical technician, serving in England, France, Belgium, and Germany. Those years of treating the wounded gave him both a toughness and a quiet compassion that marked the rest of his life.

After returning from the war, he pursued education with determination. He graduated with a degree in biology from Emmanuel Missionary College in 1952 and went on to earn a master's degree in biology from Michigan State University in 1959. Along the way, he married Bernadette in 1951, and together they raised two sons, Jay and Bradley.

He began his teaching career in the public schools of Benton Harbor, Michigan, before moving into Adventist education. In 1953 he joined Adelphian Academy in Holly, Michigan, where he taught biology and served as dean of boys. He was known as a steady leader — firm when needed, but always fair and approachable. In 1961, he became principal at Cedar Lake Academy. Six years later, he accepted the call to California to serve as principal of Loma Linda Academy. His tenure there lasted only a year, but he left his mark as a leader who could bring calm, order, and kindness to a school community.

From there he transitioned into university administration, working as a trust officer and eventually a trust administrator for the Loma Linda University Foundation. For eight years he oversaw the Real Estate Department, which managed not only local properties but holdings spread far and wide. He retired in 1987 but remained active in the community with Bernadette until the end of their lives. She passed away in April 2003, and he followed her a month later.

Those who knew him remembered his gentle humor, his quiet but firm leadership, and his dedication to helping others succeed. For me, his legacy was more personal. He was the man who took the time to meet with a high schooler he didn't even know and open a door that would shape the next decade of that young man's life. That act of kindness and encouragement made all the difference.

Chapter 43

LLU Trust Dept.

Credit: Loma Linda University Digital Archives

This chapter follows naturally after the one about Mr. Jensen, and it ties into this picture. From the time that building went up in the late fifties until I started working for the Trust Department, I knew the stores there very well. Everyone knew the post office. The bank was where my grandparents did their banking, and eventually where I did mine too. The campus cafeteria and the little snack shop in the back next to a modest food court were regular stops. The campus bookstore was there, along with the campus pharmacy.

What I didn't know then was what was going on upstairs. The second floor had the look of an office complex, but I never knew what it housed until I met Mr. Jensen. That was when I learned it was the Loma Linda University Trust Department. They were the ones who managed the donations people gave to the school, and there were plenty of those. They also handled donated property and even bought property they believed the university would need in the future. I doubt anyone working up there back then had any real idea how things would look decades later, but that's where the planning was happening.

Two people stand out to me from that place—though one of them may not have officially worked there, he was around enough that he might as well have. Those two were Ralph Kennedy and Elder Jack Bogle.

Ralph was a good man. I never did know exactly what he did before winding up at the Trust Department, but I think he had been in real estate. He seemed to know property backwards and forwards, and he acted as the real estate manager for the department whether that was his official title or not. I've always suspected it was Ralph who suggested to Mr. Jensen that he talk to me about doing electrical work, though neither one of them ever admitted it. Ralph and my grandfather had been friends for many years, both members of the Redlands Church. Ralph lived in Redlands, and my grandfather had wired that church in the late forties. After the wiring job was finished, he felt a certain obligation to transfer his membership there, and that's where the friendship began. I think they served as deacons together too.

In 1958, Ralph built a house up in the hills of Redlands. My grandfather was doing the electrical work, and as usual, he brought me along. By then I had been "working" with him since I was four. It wasn't babysitting. I crawled under houses, pulled wires, fetched tools, sorted screws and wire nuts—whatever I could handle at that age. My grandfather believed in teaching me as we went.

The Kennedy house stands out in my memory for one vivid reason. The trim was done and the power was on, and I had been given the job of testing everything. My routine was to flip switches to see if lights worked and to test outlets with my little homemade tool: a light bulb wired to two bare leads. Stick the wires in, and if the bulb lit, the outlet was hot. If it didn't, the outlet was probably on a switch.

I was going about my business when Mrs. Kennedy walked into a room just as I was plugging the bare wires into an outlet. What I remember most is the scream. A blood-curdling scream, the kind that makes your stomach twist. I didn't know she was screaming at me. For all I knew, something horrible was happening in the next room. The scream startled me so badly I dropped the bulb, which shattered on the floor. My heart pounded as I bolted for the truck, climbed into the cab, and locked the doors. I wasn't hiding from punishment—I was trying to protect myself from whatever awful thing could cause a scream like that.

Only later, after everything calmed down, did I learn she had been screaming at me, horrified to see a six-year-old sticking wires into a wall socket. My grandfather smoothed things over, explaining I knew what I was doing. From then on, he was more careful to let people know why I was there.

Years later, Ralph turned up at the Trust Department, steady as ever. It made sense. Real estate, property, responsibility—that was right in his wheelhouse.

Elder Bogle, or Jack Bogle, or J. B. as some called him, was a different kind of figure. I don't think he was there full time, but he was around the Trust Department often enough that I got to know him. He was a kind man, soft-spoken, with a genuine interest in people. I think he may have been a conference treasurer at some point, but I can't say for sure. What I can say is that he was the kind of man who left a mark quietly, without asking for recognition.

One of our casual conversations turned into something that changed my grandparents' lives. I had mentioned to him that I was living with them, and he began asking about their situation. At the time they were just going on Social Security. My grandmother was drawing a tiny pension from St. Bernardine's Hospital—ninety-nine dollars a month. Between that and Social Security, they were scraping by on maybe two or three hundred a month. Life was tight, very tight. I knew it, they knew it, but it was just the way things were.

He asked where else they had worked, and I told him about St. Bernardine's and how my grandfather had always been self-employed, so he had no retirement. Almost as an afterthought, I mentioned the years they'd both worked at New England Sanitarium. She had been a nurse; he had worked in the boiler plant, which was where he first learned the electrical trade.

"Don't they get sustentation from that?" he asked.

I didn't even know what the word meant. He explained that sustentation was the General Conference's retirement program for denominational workers. Many who had worked in the twenties and thirties never collected because they lacked proof—no records, no canceled checks, nothing left to show their employment.

Then he had an idea. Did my grandparents still know anyone from those days? If so, letters from coworkers might be enough.

As it turned out, they did. Each of them still had friends from those years. One of them was Harold Cotton from Heritage Gardens, Dan Cotton's father. So my grandparents started making calls, and soon we had a stack of letters from people who remembered working alongside them fifty years earlier.

I brought the letters to Elder Bogle, and he just said, "Let me see what I can do." He didn't promise anything.

A short time later, he called me. "Come by the office," he said. When I got there, he was smiling. "Your grandparents will start sustentation next month. They just need to fill out these forms."

It more almost quadrupled their income. The sustentation checks were far greater than Social Security and the little St. Bernardine's pension put together. Almost overnight, my grandparents went from scraping by to being comfortable. They could buy groceries without counting every dime. They could keep the thermostat where they wanted it instead of bundling up in sweaters all winter. They could even go out to dinner once in a while without feeling guilty. For the first time in years, they breathed easier.

The change was immediate in the household. My grandmother no longer fretted over every bill. My grandfather, who had carried the burden of making ends meet for so long, relaxed in a way I hadn't seen before. They could finally live the way older folks deserve to live—without fear of running out of money before the month was over.

We thanked Elder Bogle again and again, and each time he brushed it off. "It's nothing," he said. "I just helped them get what they were entitled to." That was him—humble, quiet, never seeking credit. But I'll never forget it, because he gave my grandparents something priceless: peace of mind for the rest of their days. And he gave me a memory of watching relief replace worry in the faces of two people I loved.

So when I think of that building, I think of the post office and the bank and the bookstore, but mostly I think of what was happening upstairs. That's where I met men like Ralph Kennedy, whose wife once gave me a scare I'll never forget, and Elder Jack Bogle, who gave my grandparents a future they could count on.

Chapter 44

John Burden and $38,900

Credit: Loma Linda University Digital Archives

Before there was a Loma Linda, there was a place called Mound City. About 150 years ago, it was mostly farmland, with wide stretches of orchards and vineyards tended by people who saw promise in the fertile soil. One of the biggest landowners in the area was pioneer James A. Cole, who had come to San Bernardino in 1860. His specialty was growing fruit and shipping it all the way to Arizona, which in those days was no small feat.

Mound City began with high hopes. The community had its own post office, a railroad station, and—its crown jewel—a resort hotel perched on top of the mound in 1888.

For a brief moment, it looked like the place might boom. But the post office soon closed for lack of use, and the hotel never really caught on. The railroad saw little traffic, and the developers, running out of ideas, decided to name the streets after themselves. That was about as far as the "grand plan" went.

In 1888, the San Bernardino City and County Directory offered this glowing yet strangely pessimistic description:

"A small station on the Southern Pacific Railroad, south of San Bernardino and east from Colton, received its name from the peculiar formation of the ground where it is located. A round knoll or mound here rises from the plain, comprising many acres of ground, and is prominent to view from all parts of the eastern end of the valley. Lively anticipation of this becoming a prominent town-site existed when the S.P. R.R. was first built, and a post office, store, etc., were located here. But these things have passed away and its proximity to Colton and San Bernardino preclude the probability of its ever being anything more than a possible way station."

In other words: nice place to look at, but don't get your hopes up.

The entire mound eventually fell into the hands of a wealthy private investor who tried to make something of it, planting orchards and vineyards and putting up a luxury hotel. But timing was cruel. A depression hit in 1890. Another group of investors later poured $155,000 into the project, betting big on it becoming one of California's finest health resorts. That gamble fizzled too. Not many people wanted to go to a health resort that didn't even have a working post office. So the owners decided to cut their losses. They put the whole thing on the market for $110,000. That's when John Burden came into the picture.

Burden was an Oregonian who had studied at Healdsburg College in Napa Valley, where he also met his wife. By 1888 he was working at the Rural Health Retreat, a Seventh-day Adventist sanitarium, and by 1891 he had been promoted to manager. That same year, on the urging of Merritt Kellogg—half-brother of John Harvey Kellogg, the cornflake man—Burden traveled all the way to Sydney, Australia, to help build and open another sanitarium. When he returned to California in 1904, he launched a new sanitarium in Glendale. Ellen G. White, co-founder of the Adventist church, had urged him to keep the Kelloggs out of this one, so Burden bought a $60,000 hotel for $12,500, converted it into a sanitarium, and ran it with his wife, who kept the books.

Not long after, Ellen White told Burden to check out another property—an abandoned health resort in Mound City, about 60 miles east of Glendale. Burden went to see it. He looked around and realized it was exactly what they needed. He telegraphed Ellen White with the news, and she gave the directive: get it.

There was one problem. The asking price was $110,000, and neither Burden nor the Adventist Church had that kind of money. The church was cash-strapped, and Burden himself was more used to pinching pennies than throwing around six-figure sums. Still, he began negotiating. He showed genuine interest, which turned out to be rare. The owners, desperate to sell, started dropping their price. After much back-and-forth, Burden got them down to $40,000 and secured an option on the property. Before the end of the year, he closed the deal at a final price of $38,900. In one stroke, John Burden had bought not just a hotel, but the entire town of Mound City.

He quickly reopened the sanitarium, and from there, history unfolded. The College of Medical Evangelists—what we now know as Loma Linda University—sprang up on that very ground. The post office was even reopened. What had been a failed resort town became the hub of one of the world's leading centers for health and medicine.

Burden didn't stop there. In 1915 he was sent to start another sanitarium in Paradise Valley, near San Diego. He ran it faithfully until his retirement in 1933. But he wasn't finished with Loma Linda. In 1939 he returned, this time as a chaplain and counselor. Three years later, in 1942, tragedy struck. Returning home from a Bible study in Redlands, he was involved in a traffic accident and later died from his injuries.

By then, though, the legacy was firmly in place. John Burden had taken a failed real estate venture—an entire town no one seemed to want—and turned it into something that would outlast him by generations. And he had done it for less than $40,000.

Chapter 45

The Great Flood of 1969

Photo Credit: Wheeler Photography

*A**uthor's Note: Before I begin this chapter, I want to extend special thanks to Dixie Wheeler Plata. Several years ago, while I was preparing a video about the flood, she graciously furnished me with first-generation prints made directly from the original negatives. Many of these photographs had never been shared publicly before. Dixie, who was co-owner of Wheeler Photography, provided far more material than I could include here—what you see in these pages is only a portion of her remarkable collection. To experience the full set, I've placed a QR code at the end of this chapter that links to the video where all of the images can be viewed.*

It was one of those winters that people still talk about in Southern California. The rain just would not quit. In January, it seemed like every few days another storm rolled through. Nothing extraordinary at first, just constant gray skies, puddles that grew into ponds, and the kind of cold that chills you even when you're wearing three layers. Ontario and Lytle Creek were already taking a beating by the end of that month, but folks there figured it was just another wet year. The mountains got so much snow that they closed Highway 38, the back way to Big Bear, which was never a good sign.

Then the rain stopped for a couple of weeks in early February. The sun even peeked out and people started to believe the worst was behind them. But by mid-February the skies opened up again, this time with a vengeance. I've never lived in a place where the rain came down that hard for that long, not even in Oregon where I spent thirty years. Ten days brought almost a foot of warm rain, the kind that melts snow in the mountains. That was the deadly combination—rain coming down while snowpack turned to runoff at the same time. San Timoteo Creek and every other wash in the Inland Empire swelled to their breaking point.

The first roads to go were Orange Street between Redlands and Highland, then Alabama Street. Before long, everywhere you tried to drive seemed underwater. It was attrition. One road after another fell, until the only safe routes were higher ground. By the last week of February, it was obvious something big was about to break.

Photo Credit: Wheeler Photography

On Tuesday, February 25, it did. I was living in Mentone then, going to school in Redlands, and working in Yucaipa. That morning I crossed Anderson and saw a crowd standing on the bridge just watching the torrent below. School barely got started before it was cancelled and everyone was sent home. I didn't go straight back—I was too curious. I went back to that bridge and watched the river tearing everything in its path apart. First came piles of wood debris, then entire trees, then the unthinkable: a house floating down like it had been plucked from its foundation. Not long after that, another bridge—still wrapped in its railings and supports—came bobbing down like a raft.

That was enough to shake me. I ran across the Anderson Bridge just as they closed it to traffic, jumped into my VW van, and tried to make my way home. Easier said than done. Barton Road was shut down at Bryn Mawr. Mount View was under water. Waterman at Redlands Boulevard was flooded. I kept chasing a way west but every route seemed cut off. Finally, I made it through Grand Terrace and hit the freeway. Because the freeway had been built up higher, it was one of the few safe passages. From there I made it to the University offramp in Redlands, cut through side streets, skirted around the flooded Zanja, and at last reached Mentone. It felt like I'd run a gauntlet.

Photo Credit: Wheeler Photography

By Thursday the rain had let up, so I headed back toward Loma Linda to see the damage. What I found was heartbreaking. The town was torn up. Two-thirds of Loma Linda had been flooded. The Academy was under water, and when the water receded the cleanup job seemed endless. Students pitched in with brooms, shovels, and whatever else they could get their hands on. We weren't professionals, but we were there.

That morning, just as everyone was finally making progress, panic struck again. Sheriff's deputies came barreling in, yelling that we needed to run for our lives. A dam had broken, they said, and a twenty-foot wall of water was racing down from Oak Glen straight at us. We bolted. Hundreds of us scrambled up onto the new Anderson bridge over the railroad tracks, hearts pounding, waiting to see a wall of water come roaring down. We stood there for two hours, waiting, until the word finally filtered through that it was a false alarm. The dam hadn't broken at all. It was just another rumor that spread faster than the flood itself.

Photo Credit: Wheeler Photography

When the panic lifted, we went back to work. My friend Eddie and I got assigned to cleanup duty in the basement. Eddie and I were known for being, well, pranksters, and sure enough, temptation got the better of us that day. We stumbled across our English teacher Mrs. Magi's gradebook, the pages smeared and smudged with water damage. Eddie showed me how easy it was to change a D+ into a B+ in those wet pages. I went along with it, though I'll admit it here and now—it wasn't my proudest moment. Years later, I told Mrs. Magi the story. She laughed, shook her head, and gave me the gentlest kind of absolution a former student could hope for. "You turned out fine," she said.

School stayed closed for two full weeks. About four days after the flood, I got a call from my friend Howard Conklin. He owned a backhoe and had gone up to Dunlap Acres in Yucaipa to help a buddy dig out. Once people saw him working, everyone in the neighborhood wanted help. Howard was about to buy a new JWB backhoe anyway, so he offered me a chance to run his old one for five dollars an hour. That was good money in 1969, and I jumped on it.

For the next month, we worked side by side, cleaning out basements, yards, and driveways that had been swallowed by mud. Howard made so much money with two machines running that he had the new one paid off in a month. I remember working long days on that backhoe, listening to KFXM radio blasting from the cab. The soundtrack of that muddy cleanup included songs like "Day After Day," which had a line about California falling into the ocean, "Proud Mary," and "Ramblin' Gamblin' Man." I gave Howard that last nickname because he'd bought his new backhoe on the gamble that work would keep coming.

Photo Credit: Wheeler Photography

Howard wasn't just making money—he showed a side of himself that left an impression on me. He told people not to worry about paying until they got their insurance checks. For folks who had no insurance, he often did the work for free. That's the kind of thing you don't forget.

The devastation was staggering. In the Inland Empire, at least two people drowned. All across Southern California, 115 lives were lost to the winter of '69. Six counties were declared federal disaster areas. The February storm alone caused more than 30 million dollars in damages in San Bernardino County, which was no small figure back then. Statewide, the toll was closer to 200 million, and those are 1969 dollars. Adjusted for today, it was billions.

For Loma Linda, the beating came straight from San Timoteo Creek. The creek was usually a trickle, the kind of place kids might poke around for frogs in the summer. But in February of '69, it transformed into a monster. Bridges were washed away like twigs. Streets vanished. Homes filled with water and mud. The Academy had waterlines halfway up the walls, classrooms ruined, and basements filled with sludge. Students and faculty rolled up their sleeves and became janitors overnight.

Photo Credit: Wheeler Photography

I can still see the image of people crowding the bridges, staring down at the torrent with awe and fear. There's something hypnotic about watching a river carry away pieces of civilization—fences, cars, furniture, entire trees. It reminded you how fragile our little human projects are when nature decides to flex its muscles.

After the waters receded, Loma Linda was a different place. For weeks you could still smell the dampness in every building. Lawns were buried under silt. Streets were gouged and scarred. The cleanup went on for months. The San

Bernardino County Flood Control District later called the Flood of '69 one of the defining events of its history, one that reshaped how the region thought about flood channels, levees, and creek management. It forced upgrades to infrastructure that are still protecting people today.

But in the middle of all those big numbers and reports, there were the little moments. Kids who treated a flooded playground like an adventure. Neighbors who showed up with shovels to help strangers dig out. People who shared food and blankets with families whose houses were unlivable. Even Eddie and I, gradebook mischief aside, spent hours hauling ruined furniture and mud-soaked boxes out of classrooms.

Photo Credit: Wheeler Photography

Looking back now, fifty-five years later, the flood sits in my memory as a mix of awe, fear, mischief, and community. It was terrifying to see bridges ripped from their moorings and whole houses floating downstream. It was exhausting to clean up endless mud and debris. It was humbling to realize how small we are against a storm. And yet, it was also inspiring to see people rally together, to watch a town like Loma Linda refuse to be washed away.

The Flood of '69 wasn't just an event—it was an education. It taught me respect for water, for nature, and for community. It gave me my first taste of running heavy equipment for pay, and it introduced me to the kind of generosity that people like Howard showed when times were tough. It gave me stories I'm still telling today, more than half a century later.

Photo Credit: Wheeler Photography

When you see the old black-and-white photos in the archives, with cars buried up to their windows and kids in rubber boots sloshing through streets that look like rivers, it can feel like a different world. But for those of us who lived it, the memories are as sharp as yesterday. The sound of rain on the roof that winter. The shock of seeing a bridge floating past. The panic on the Anderson overpass when we all thought a wall of water was coming. The music on the radio as we dug out. The laughter when Eddie turned D's into B's with a smear of mud. The smell of wet books and ruined classrooms. The relief of sunshine breaking through at last.

It was a season of disaster, but also of resilience. And if you drive through Loma Linda today, past the Academy, past the bridges over San Timoteo, past the neighborhoods that once sat underwater, you'd never guess how close the town came to being washed away in 1969. But those of us who remember can tell you—it was a flood like no other.

Chapter 46

I (also) Remember Loma Linda

By: Nancy Magi

I REMEMBER LOMA LINDA

Mrs. Nancy Magi
English, Speech
Journalism
"Mirror"

Photo Credit: The Lomasphere

(***Authors' Note:*** *I may be one of the few left who still calls her "Mrs. Magi," but that's because it's the way I've always thought of her—with respect, both as a teacher and as a person. She wasn't much older than us, but at the Academy she was the "cool" teacher. Her patience seemed endless, and she had a way of making every student feel like she truly cared.*

During my junior and senior years at Loma Linda, school wasn't always my highest priority. But Mrs. Magi's classes were different. They were the ones we looked forward to every single day. Even when I skipped other classes, I'd still show up for her speech and journalism class because it was fun, engaging, and felt like it mattered.

Looking back, I know I could have treated her better. I was a bit of a smart aleck teenager, but she always rose to the challenge and never let my antics get in the way. She had a quiet strength about her, and she knew how to bring out the best in us, even when we didn't make it easy.

For me, the years 1967, 1968, and 1969 were the best years of my life—and Mrs. Magi was right at the center of them. I'll always be grateful for the way she taught, the way she cared, and the way she made school something to look forward to. Thank you, Mrs. Magi—you made a bigger difference than I ever told you back then.)

When Enn and I drove our little Corvair across the country to California, we weren't entirely sure what we were doing. We had left the East Coast without air conditioning, rolling down the windows and fanning ourselves in the summer heat. By the time we reached Loma Linda, we were hot, tired, and a little overwhelmed, but also full of hope. We were young, ready to begin, and trusting that somehow things would fall into place.

One of the first signs that we had landed in the right spot came at the very first gathering for the Class of 1970. Dr. Hadley walked up to us, introduced himself, and immediately called us by name. I still don't know how he did it, but he had a gift for remembering faces and stories. That small gesture meant the world to me. It told me that even though we were far from home, there were people here who cared and who would make sure we didn't feel alone.

Our first home was a duplex on Anderson Street, found for us by my aunt and uncle. The house is still standing today, though the lawn that once stretched out front has long since been paved into a parking lot. Back then, though, it was green and welcoming. We filled the place with the little we had—some boxes, some second-hand furniture, and wedding gifts—and called it home.

My first teaching assignment was not at Loma Linda Academy, but at La Sierra Junior Academy. The conference had hired me sight unseen to teach seventh grade English. That year was, to put it gently, miserable. I didn't know how to manage a classroom, and though the students seemed to like me, it was only because they could take advantage of me. I would drive home from La Sierra every day exhausted and discouraged, wondering if perhaps I should abandon teaching altogether and try something else, maybe even real estate. I promised myself that if I were ever given another chance, I would not make the same mistakes.

That second chance came quickly. The following summer, I was hired at Loma Linda Academy. The principal who took me on was Herluf Jensen. He had come from Adelphian Academy in Michigan, a very conservative boarding school, and he was, in many ways, a traditionalist. But he gave me the opportunity I needed. I decided right then and there that I was going to start my first year at the Academy differently. I would set the tone from day one. For the first few weeks, I hardly smiled. I was firm, direct, and left no room for nonsense. The students whispered among themselves that I was mean, and I thought, "Good. Now we can learn." And we did. By the time I relaxed and allowed myself to be more open, the groundwork had been laid, and we were able to build something good together.

During my interview, Dr. Branson had asked me to make sure that the students read Shakespeare. That had not always been encouraged, but he believed it was important. The anthology we were using contained Macbeth, so that became our play. It was the first time I had taught Shakespeare, and the first time the students had read him. We discovered it together, puzzling through the language and marveling at the story. Those classes remain some of my fondest memories.

Floods were not common in Loma Linda, but the flood of 1969 was frightening. Water came rushing down so quickly that I thought for sure our little place on Court Street was going to be ruined. We had moved there from Anderson Street because the rent was cheaper—fifteen dollars less each month—and the building was owned by Cliff and Lucy Coffin of Loma Linda Automotive. They were wonderful people who gave us what I still think of as the deal of the century: seventy dollars a month, two dollars a day, and they never once raised it. During the flood, it was their daughter and her husband who came to our rescue. They dug up sod and laid down beach towels to divert the water, and somehow it worked. Our apartment stayed dry. That quick action saved us from disaster, and it showed the kind of neighbors we were surrounded by in Loma Linda.

Photo Credit: Nancy Magi

After the flood, the church took up a collection for teachers who had lost personal belongings. With that money, Enn and I bought a harpsichord kit. Enn was in the middle of his surgery rotation, yet at night he would come home and carefully assemble the instrument piece by piece. Students would stop by just to see it, curious about the project. The Schwantz family even borrowed it for performances, carrying it out carefully and always returning it in good condition. That harpsichord was more than just a musical instrument; it became a symbol of creativity and resilience during those years.

My colleagues at the Academy made the work even more rewarding. Mr. Olmstead was someone I could always talk to when I needed advice or encouragement. Herb Johns respected the work I did and was supportive in quiet but important ways. Mr. Shepard, the chemistry teacher, had a remarkable personal story and carried himself with dignity and kindness. And Barbara Powers became a lifelong friend.

The students, of course, were what made each day worth it. They were clever, energetic, and often full of surprises. I'll never forget the day Ken Nelson arrived at my home in full scuba gear, flippers and snorkel included, announcing that he needed to inspect the plumbing. He even stood in the bathtub to make the performance complete. It was hilarious and harmless, exactly the kind of mischief that brightened my days. There were other pranks too—Easter eggs hidden in odd places, toilet paper in trees, little jokes that made me laugh more than anything else. They were good kids.

Our principal, Herluf Jensen, left after just one year, but during that time we became well acquainted since my classroom was right next to his office. He was very proper and careful, and one day he called me in to tell me my skirts were too short because when I leaned over at the chalkboard, he could see the fasteners on my stockings. These were the days before pantyhose, when women wore girdles or garter belts. He didn't actually use those words—he was far too modest—but we both knew what he meant. It was awkward for both of us, but looking back, it makes me smile. It was simply the clash of two different worlds, both trying to adjust.

Life in Loma Linda itself was lovely. The orange groves were everywhere, and in the evenings the whole town seemed to carry the scent of blossoms. You don't get that anymore, except if you stand right next to your own tree, but back then it was everywhere. It's a smell that still comes back to me when I think of those days.

Kindness seemed to surround us. The Rosenquist family, especially Betty, treated us like family. We were often invited into their home, and their daughter Diane and son Robert became close friends. Robert was also one of my students, and like Mike and a few others, he is someone I have never forgotten.

Miss McBroom, the librarian, and I worked together when I supervised study hall, though I never felt entirely confident about maintaining order in that setting. I still remember the nervousness I felt during chapel duty, worried that a marble or BB would roll across the floor. It seems small now, but at the time I carried that responsibility heavily.

The years went by quickly. In 1970, Enn and I both graduated at the same ceremony at the Redlands Bowl. He received his medical degree, and I received my master's degree in English. To stand there together, each of us reaching such a milestone, was one of the proudest nights of my life.

Time moved on, and for many years I lost touch with the students and colleagues who had filled those days. Then, out of the blue, I received an email from Mike. He asked if I remembered him. I laughed when I read it, because of course I did. That one email opened the door to reconnecting with so many of my former students. From there, it spread to Facebook, where messages and stories began flowing back and forth. I pulled out my old yearbooks before reunions, studying the names and faces so I would be ready. Walking into those gatherings was like stepping back in time. The students remembered me more warmly than I ever imagined, and the memories came flooding back as though no time had passed at all.

Those three years in Loma Linda were brief in number but deep in meaning. They gave me students who made me laugh, colleagues who supported me, neighbors who cared for us, and friends who became family. They gave me the smell of orange blossoms, the laughter of young people, and the reassurance that even far from home, we belonged. And years later, thanks to one email and the ripple effect of Facebook, they gave me the gift of living those memories all over again.

Index

A

Academy Fire (Loma Linda Academy, 1947), 38
Adventist Church (first congregation on the hill), 35
Adventist Health principles (vegetarianism, diet, exercise), 28, 41
Air Force Bases (Norton, March, El Toro), 40
Alta (sister of Lupe; Lupe's Mexican Restaurant), 33
Anderson Street Overpass (completed 1968; view of LLU UFO), 30
Anderson Street (hospital move 1967, Army convoy), 40
Apple pie (Law's Coffee Shop, Wallace Koehl ritual), 34
Apartments (Mitchell rental units; Yucaipa grove), 29, 34

B

Bailey, Leonard (heart transplant surgeon; mentored by Wareham), 26
Bakeries (Mitchell's Alfa-Rice, sourdough smell), 29
Barton Road (Emenel building; LLU UFO view; Hulda Crooks Park), 29, 30, 41
Basketball (games at Gentry Gym), 30
Ben-Hur (Movieland Wax Museum chariot scene, Gene

White), 32
Bible (tiny red Bible in vegetable truck, Mr. Perkins), 27
BFI – Browning Ferris Industries (acquired Loma Linda Disposal, 1989), 36
Blue Zones longevity (Hulda Crooks, Ellsworth Wareham), 26, 41
Burden, Pastor (site selection committee for La Sierra), 38
Bus rides (hospital patients moved by Army Reserve, 1967), 40

C

Calico Mine Ride (Knott's Berry Farm, Gene White), 32
Caltrans (purchased Koehl's garage property; I-10), 34
Campus Snack Shop (LLU downtown; Postum, veggie burgers), 37
Casa de Vikki (Mentone; same family as Lupe's), 33
Central Avenue (Unger's station, court), 25
Ceroplex vitamins (Mitchell formula, 33 ingredients), 29
Cheeseburger ban (Campus Snack Shop menu), 37
Cherry Valley (farm produce for vegetable truck), 27
Chile (Heart Team missions), 26
China (Heart Team missions), 26
Choirs, vespers (Heritage Gardens, Cotton family), 22
Cliburn, Van (concert at Gentry Gym), 30
Cloverleaf Towers (nickname of new LLU Hospital, 1967), 40
Coke ban (Campus Snack Shop rules), 37
Colton (railroad tracks to lab; hospital rides to Indians), 35, 28
Colton (tri-city junction with LL and SB; Emenel site), 29
Community Hospital, Loma Linda (Cotton family; later

East Campus), 22
Computer system (1967, linked LLU and UCLA, proto-internet), 40
Cotton family (Dan, Patti, Jenny; Heritage Gardens, hospital), 22
Crooks, Dr. Samuel (husband of Hulda; physician in Loma Linda), 41
Crooks, Hulda (aka "Grandma Whitney," hiker, LLU dietitian, 1927), 41
Crooks Peak (Whitney spire renamed in her honor, 1990), 41

D

Dale Gentry (California Hotel, LLU UFO gymnasium donor), 30
Dancing towers (earthquake absorbers; LLU hospital 1967), 40
Day Needle (Whitney spire; renamed Crooks Peak), 41
Dental School (LLU; replaced Harlow's store, 1960s), 35
Digneo, Elmer (Councilman; friend of Clarence Harlow), 35
Disposal, Loma Linda (founded 1957; Robert; later sold to BFI), 36
Don McCoy (DJ; started at KDUO, later #1 at KFXM), 19
Dry cleaning delivery (porch pickup and return), 27

E

East Campus (former Loma Linda Community Hospital), 22
Edison (electrical work, Koehl, Harlow), 34, 35

Eisenhower High School (pool built by Stan Nelson), 23
Electricity fear (Hulda Crooks calling Amos for help), 41
El Toro Marine Station (ambulances for hospital move), 40
Emmerson, Richard F. (Dick; La Sierra site purchase, mortuary founder), 38
Emmerson Mortuary (Redlands; later Bartlett-Emmerson), 38
Emenel (Dan Mitchell's supplement company; Barton R d.), 29

F

Fennel seed (ingredient in Sofcol laxative), 29
Flood of 1969 (hospital gym shelter), 30
Food deliveries (vegetable truck, Helms Bakery, milkman, ice cream truck), 27
Forest Service (Jim Slater, early job at age 14), 24
Fuller Brush man (door-to-door sales), 27
Fuji, Mount (Japan; climbed by Hulda Crooks at age 91), 41

G

Gentry Gym (LLU geodesic dome, "UFO"), 30
George, Dr. Lyra (LLU faculty, obstetrician, Serrano tribes, San Manuel support), 28
Grand opening (Harlow store 1964, Tippecanoe), 35
Grandchildren (Judge Unger legacy), 25

H

Harlow, Clarence (ice delivery, appliance dealer, civic leader), 35

Harlow's Appliance Store (downtown, later Tippecanoe, 1964), 35
Helms Bakery (yellow truck, cookies, pastries), 27
Heritage Gardens (Cotton family facility), 22
Hiking (Whitney, John Muir Trail, Hulda Crooks), 41
Hulda Crooks Park (Loma Linda, named in her honor, bronze statue), 41

I

Ice delivery (Clarence Harlow, 1920s), 35
Indians, Serrano (Dr. George horseback trips; gratitude to LLU), 28
Internet precursor (LLU–UCLA computer link, 1967), 40
In-N-Out (Tippecanoe, memory of Wallace Koehl garage site), 34

J

Japan (Fuji climb by Hulda Crooks), 41
Jerry Lewis (Congressman; Crooks Peak renaming), 41
John Muir Trail (completed by Hulda Crooks), 41
Judge Van Unger (gas station, Justice of the Peace, Pathfinder, Mexico mission), 25

K

Kauai steam locomotive (owned by Dale Gentry, moved to High Desert ranch), 30
Kingsley, Bill (General Telephone supervisor; prank on new hires at Campus Snack Shop), 37
Koehl, Wallace (garage fire, peach grove, Yucaipa), 34
Knott's Berry Farm (Calico Mine Ride, Log Ride; Gene

White), 32
KDUO (FM radio station, "Do Unto Others," later KLYY José 97.5), 19

L

La Habra (W.J. Hole ranch), 38
La Sierra (site chosen for school instead of Yucaipa), 38
Law's Coffee Shop (apple pie ritual, Koehl), 34
Lemonade (Campus Snack Shop menu option), 37
Lencho (Lupe's husband; multitasker, Kit Kat sales), 33
Log Ride (Knott's; Gene White project), 32
Loma Linda Academy (fire of 1947), 38
Loma Linda Bulletin (hospital approval 1971), 22
Loma Linda Chamber of Commerce (founded 1959; Harlow), 35
Loma Linda Disposal (Robert's company, 1957–1989), 36
Loma Linda University (history, towers, faculty, heart team), 26, 28, 40

M

Mac McGurr (pool manager, strict suit rules), 31
March Air Force Base (ambulances, hospital move), 40
Marineland (inspired Stan Nelson's wall of water pool), 23
Maytag (appliances sold by Harlow), 35
Mentone (Lupe's; Koehl ranch neighbor; SAC Health expansion), 33, 34, 28
Mitchell, Dan (Emenel supplements founder, Alfa-Rice, Barton Rd.), 29
Mortuary, Emmerson (Redlands, later Bartlett-Emmer-

son), 38
Moving Day (hospital move, July 9, 1967, Army-led), 40
Muir Trail (see John Muir Trail), 41
Music concerts (Van Cliburn, 1812 Overture at Gentry Gym), 30
Magi, Nancy, 274–280

N

Nelson, Stan (built pool with glass wall; lifeguard at Unger's mission trips), 23, 25
Nelson, Genie (story of wall of water pool), 23
Norton Air Force Base (Quonset hut to Emenel; vehicles for hospital move), 29, 40

O

Orange groves (Dr. George's trees; Hulda Crooks Park), 28, 41
Orinda-Moraga Disposal (Robert, post-Loma Linda Disposal scandal), 36

P

Pathfinder Club (Judge Unger, Loma Linda), 25
Peach groves (Koehl's Yucaipa property), 34
Perkins, Mr. (vegetable truck driver), 27
Peterson, Robert (pool lifeguard, 1967), 31
Piano concert (Van Cliburn at Gentry Gym), 30
Platner, Wallace (hospital move organizer), 40
Plunge (Loma Linda pool, Aunt Betty, Robert Peterson), 31
Postum (Campus Snack Shop beverage; Adventist alternative), 37

Q

Quonset hut (ex-Air Force; reused for Emenel factory), 29

R

Reagan, Ronald (letter to Hulda Crooks), 41
Redlands Blvd. (Lupe's location; Hwy 99), 33
Redlands, Richard Emmerson (mortuary; La Sierra site search), 38
Reidar Schmidt (pool lifeguard, auto racing fan), 31
Rock rides (Knott's; Gene White sculpting), 32

S

SAC Health System (descendant of Social Action Corps, 1960s–present), 28
San Manuel Band of Mission Indians (support for LLU, $25m gift), 28
San Marcos & San Mateo corner (Dr. George home, orange trees), 28
San Mateo Street (vegetable truck stop; Dr. George's home), 27, 28
School of Dentistry (LLU; replaced Harlow's store), 35
Sears catalog (mail order, "printed Amazon"), 27
Servel refrigerators (gas; Harlow's sales contest), 35
Slater, Dr. James M. (proton therapy, LLUMC), 24
Slater family (film footage; QR code), 24
Smitty (barber; "wire brush haircut" joke about Dan Mitchell), 29
Social Action Corps (1960s student-run free clinic, Dr. George legacy), 28
Sofcol (Mitchell laxative, 1952), 29
Steam locomotive (Dale Gentry, Kauai to National Orange

Show), 30
Student traditions (Campus Snack Shop stories, new hires), 37

T

Tennis courts (next to Loma Linda pool, Aunt Betty memories), 31
Terminal Island Naval Station (vehicles for hospital move), 40
Tupperware (door-to-door saleswomen), 27
Typing pools (Hospital computer system, early "internet"), 40

U

Unger, Judge Van (Justice of the Peace; Pathfinder; mission builder), 25
University Mobile Estates (Gene White cabin, spa), 32
University of Utah (Jim Slater physics degree, 1955), 24
U.S. Army (Reserve, led hospital move 1967), 40
U.S. Presidents (Reagan, Bush letters to Hulda Crooks), 41
UFO (nickname for Gentry Gym dome), 30

V

Valle de la Trinidad, Mexico (Unger/Nelson Pathfinder mission project), 25
Vegetable truck (Mr. Perkins, Yucaipa farms, 1950s deliveries), 27
Vollmer, Dr. Henry (committee with Emmerson, Burden, La Sierra site), 38

W

Wall of Water (Stan Nelson pool with glass side), 23
Wallace Koehl (garage fire, I-10 sale, Yucaipa grove), 34
Wareham, Dr. Ellsworth (LLU Heart Team founder, surgeon, longevity), 26
Whitney, Mount (Hulda Crooks' 23 ascents, ages 66–91), 41
Wig store cave (Gene White design, Central City Mall), 32
World War II (Wareham, surgeon; 349th Army Hospital move), 26, 40
WWII refugee support (Vietnamese refugees, Gentry Gym shelter), 30
W.J. Hole (rancher, La Sierra property sale), 38

Y

Yucaipa (Koehl's peach grove; site nearly chosen for college), 34, 38

www.ingramcontent.com/pod-product-compliance
Lightning Source LLC
Chambersburg PA
CBHW022026050526
44107CB00125B/1452/J